CAREERS AND CONTINGENCIES

CAREERS AND CONTINGENCIES

How College Women Juggle With Gender

SHIRLEY S. ANGRIST *and* ELIZABETH M. ALMQUIST

Foreword by Jessie Bernard

DUNELLEN

New York • London

HD
6095
.A674

International Standard Book Number 8046-7100-1
Library of Congress Catalogue Card Number ~~73-88666~~ *wrong #*
Printed in the United States of America   75-326795

UNIVERSITY PRESS OF CAMBRIDGE, MASS SERIES
CONSULTING EDITOR: EUGENE H. NELLEN

Contents

Acknowledgements

The longitudinal study of college women described in this book was generously supported by a grant from Ms. Alan M. Scaife. In addition, during 1968-69 the senior author was a Research Affiliate of the Radcliffe Institute and benefitted from the support and stimulating contact with staff members and especially the late Constance Smith. The study itself and the preparation of this book were facilitated by many people. We owe special thanks to E. R. Steinberg, B. J. Lloyd and W. W. Cooper for their help with resources and encouragement. We are grateful to the late Edward R. Suchman and Douglas Stewart for advice on the study design and data analysis. We appreciate the help provided by Walter Abel, Benjamin Kleinmuntz and Robert Morgan during the data collection stage of the research. Because the study lasted through four years of data collection with additional years of data analysis and writing, we owe thanks to many research assistants: Laura Searls, Virginia Schenck, Lois Leech, Joan Kovalic, Lorna Hershberger Curran, Joanne Friedman, Susan Haynes Pepper, Marcia Karlek Millmore, David Harris, James Williams, Judith Litman, Kay Crawford, Clara Kline, Forest Jewell, Cleo Dawson.

We are grateful to the many University staff and faculty who assisted us through providing information and effort for the benefit of the research. We especially thank students who willingly participated in this study.

We appreciate the useful comments and criticisms from several colleagues who read the manuscript at various stages: Charles Bonjean, Jessie Bernard, Betty Jane Lloyd, Sara Beth Nerlove, Erwin R. Steinberg and Judy Tully. The book benefitted greatly from their advice, but we take sole responsibility for any faults which it retains.

We thank Marjorie Grabek for her patience and excellent typing in preparation of the manuscript. To Ed Fisher, Jr. we express our gratitude for his fine design of the Figures in Chapter 3.

We want to acknowledge the following for permission to use materials from articles previously published by the authors:

Sociology and Social Research, Shirley S. Angrist, "Role Conception as a Predictor of Adult Female Roles," in volume 50, July 1966, pp. 448-459.

Academic Press, Inc., publishers of the *Journal of Vocational Behavior*, Elizabeth M. Almquist, "Sex Stereotypes in Occupational Choice: The Case for College Women", in press.

American Personnel and Guidance Association, publishers of *The Journal of College Student Personnel*, Shirley S. Angrist, "Counseling College Women About Careers", November 1972, pp. 494-498.

Society for The Psychological Study of Social Issues, publishers of *The Journal of Social Issues*, Shirley S. Angrist, "The Study of Sex Roles", volume 25, January 1969, pp. 215-232.

International Journal of Sociology of the Family, Shirley S. Angrist, "Changes in Women's Work Aspirations During College", volume 2, March 1972, pp. 1-11.

Sociological Symposium, Shirley S. Angrist, "Personality Maladjustment and Career Aspirations of College Women", No. 5, Fall 1970, pp. 1-8.

Merrill-Palmer Institute, publishers of the *Merrill-Palmer*

Quarterly of Behavior and Development, Elizabeth M. Almquist and Shirley S. Angrist, "Role Model Influences on College Women's Career Aspirations", volume 17, No. 3, 1971, pp. 263-279.

North Central Sociological Association, publishers of *Sociological Focus*, Shirley S. Angrist, "Measuring Women's Career Commitment", volume 5, No. 2, Winter 1971-72, pp. 29-39.

National Council on Family Relations, publishers of the *Journal of Marriage and the Family*, Elizabeth M. Almquist and Shirley S. Angrist, "Career Salience and Atypicality of Occupational Choice Among College Women", volume 32, May 1970, pp. 242-249; and Shirley S. Angrist, "Variations in Women's Adult Aspirations During College", volume 34, August 1972, pp. 465-468; and Shirley S. Angrist, "Reply to Dr. McCord, Letters to the Editor", volume 35, August 1973, pp. 389-390.

Finally, we acknowledge our husbands and children without whom this book would have been finished sooner!

Foreword

by
JessieBernard

No one knew in 1964—when the young women whose story is recounted here entered college—that we were on the threshold of one of the most disturbed, even explosive, periods of our history. Civil rights, the Vietnam war, burning cities, anti-war marches, a war on poverty, a string of spectacular court decisions. . . . All this and more seemed to pound at the very foundations of the status quo. On campuses a silent college generation had been followed by an activist, not to say revolutionary, one. A counter-culture surfaced with an ideology that turned the most cherished tenets of our traditional ethos inside out.

Young women were going through equally momentous, though as yet less spectacular, changes themselves. The era of the feminine mystique was coming to an end: just three years earlier the long dormancy of the women's movement had begun to stir; the proportion of freshmen classes who were women was beginning to rise; young women were beginning to be rebuked for the post-war retreat into domesticity;[1] career women were beginning to recoup the loss in prestige they had suffered in preceding decades;[2] marriage was beginning to find competition from other interests; the first-marriage rate continued the decline which had begun in the mid-forties;[3] the birth rate had begun to decline in the late 50s. As the authors of this book say, "in both time and place, the sample was special and unique." By the time they finished college the trends that in 1964 had been only dimly perceived if at all were beginning to clarify. A wholly new perspective on the status of women was being articulated. A wholly new vocabulary was becoming available to think about it. The college years of the young women here reported on were years of gestation for revolutionary ideas, concepts, ideologies. No wonder, as the authors tell us, they were "a special mix of the old and the new . . . neither solidly traditional nor patently pioneer in their outlook." By 1967, the entering students already "began to look less traditional." We are lucky to have this painstaking study of the impact of all these changes on this transitional generation.

Within the sheltered walls of a technically oriented university, itself in throes of reorientation, the 87 women who are the "heroines" of this story—born in 1948 and hence socialized in the heyday of the era of the feminine mystique—began a four-year intellectual odyssey. Young women like them were entering all kinds of colleges everywhere in the country. And all of them, different in as many ways as one can think of, were going to wrestle with exactly the same contingencies.

This welcome book is one of a growing number that attempt to overcome what I have called the Pickwick fallacy. (Mr. Pickwick, called upon to write a paper on Chinese metaphysics, read everything in the encyclopedia on China and everything on metaphysics and was thus well qualified to write on Chinese metaphysics). There are substantial bodies of research on occupational choices among women and on family roles, but only now are we coming really to integrate the two. Thus the present study, with its "total view", deals with *life styles*, a concept that sees both the work and the family roles as integrally related. There was a time when college women seriously debated the marriage-versus-career dilemma. It was taken for granted that they could not possibly have both. When Alice Freeman married it was just assumed she would resign the presidency of Wellesley College. Vida Scudder, also of Wellesley, seriously presented the career option, pointing out the costs and benefits of both. The marriage rate for career women was low. Even when it became acceptable for women to have both marriage and outside work, it had to be only a job, not a commitment. Now they can have not only both marriage and a job but also both children and a job. And, as the present study shows, we are well on our way to making it acceptable to have both children and a career. The life style approach transcends the old formulation of women's choices. Now it is the timing rather than the choice that becomes the issue.

Occupational choices have to be made no matter what life style one selects. Young men, of course, also have to wrestle with career problems. But their's are more unidimensional in the sense that only their careers are involved, not total life styles; and colleges and universities know the hazards. Even if they cannot help the student overcome all of them, at least they know the course and what is par for it. Young women have more than career choices to wrestle with and colleges and universities are not well prepared even to help think them through, let alone cooperate in solving them. For, as the authors so well remind us, all the plans young women make are contingent upon the kind of marriages they will have.

Until recently there was less uncertainty than there is now about the kind of marriage young women would have. They knew in general what kind of marriage they were likely to have. And even if it were limited, the payoff for women was less than for men, opportunities for advancement were restricted, prestige was low; the payoff for vicarious achievement by way of husband's career was often higher than achievement by way of one's own. "Thus the socially rewarded alternatives to marriage [were] limited for women. In terms of role gratification, the most socially available avenue to a rewarding career . . . appeared to be marriage—particularly when marriage [could] be combined with a job, as opposed to a career."[4]

Young women today can no longer be as sure about the kind of marriage they will have as they once could. And they seem to be in a thoughtful re-appraisal of their options. For the first five months of 1974, for example, the total marriage rate was down 4.3 percent over 1973. This means that young women were at least delaying marriage, if not foregoing it entirely. And those who were married were having fewer babies; the fertility rate for the year ending May, 1974, was 5 percent lower than for the year ending May, 1973.[5] Something was competing with marriage and children for the time and attention of women. And at least some of the young women in the present study who probably married in the late 60s were doubtless among those who contributed to the 5 percent increase in the divorce rate for the first five months of 1974 over 1973.

What could we expect if we had models of marriage in which role-sharing was taken for granted? In which the costs of careers were not so heavy for mothers? In which young women took it for granted that they had as much responsibility for child-rearing as women and young women, took it for granted that they had as much responsibility as men to "provide"? It would certainly change the contingencies. Would it make career choices easier? The authors quote Mirra Komarovsky's recent study of college men to document the inconsistencies men themselves are experiencing (p. 37). It will take some time before marriage accommodates itself to the new demands being made on it.

One of the most remarkable findings of this study is the fact that, with the odds so heavily against them—and the authors leave us in no doubt about the odds—almost a fifth of the young women they studied have opted for careers. And more than a fifth, became converted. The young women who are career oriented are extraordinarily interesting. The authors successfully refute the old cliche that they are "deviant." Different they certainly are: but the old interpretation of them as misfits is certainly not valid. Ravenna Helson concurs. Like the present authors, she has reviewed the research literature and found it inadequate. The present study is one that, in Helson's words, seeks "to work through the idea that women can participate fully and equally in what men have regarded their world."[6]

The term "role transcenders" has been suggested for those who overcome the limits set by sex-role stereotyping.[7] On the basis of the annual survey data gathered by the American Council on Education, Engin Holstrom and I have found that young women who are "role transcenders" are more "masculine" than men in life goals considered essential or very important, but also more "feminine" than other women.[8]

The data on careerists, converts, shifters, non-careerists, and defectors are especially interesting because they help answer a question that often arises in mixed-sex conference groups: what sex composition should we aim at in any given occupation? What could we expect if no occupations were sex-typed? When neither sex is "programmed" for given occupations? When individual talent and motivation rather than sex determine the occupational distribution for both sexes? How would it differ from the present? If there were neither intrinsic nor extrinsic sex-based barriers to any of the professions, would the proportion of women choosing any given profession be the same as the proportion of men? As yet we do not know. The socialization of the sexes still precludes the selection of certain careers for both sexes. But if almost a fifth of college seniors would choose preponderantly male-type careers, what proportion would do so without present obstacles?[9]

The authors of this valuable book do not just stand there. They want to do something to make true options available for college women, to remove both the intrinsic forces that so drastically limit them now. They offer ideas on how professions, counselors, and parents can help. They make suggestions for what colleges can do. And they tell young women what they can do.

I am particularly touched by the special appeal they make at the end of the book to their "spiritual daughters" whom they must have come to know well as they sat through all those interview-hours over four years. As scientists throughout the book they have presented their data. Now in the home stretch, their concern for the young women is allowed to shine through. One catches a glimpse of the yearning that must have informed the research as they watched their subjects wrestling with the major questions they were having to deal with. "You can! You can!" they seem to be saying. "Don't set your sights too low!" I feel very much the same way. The young women can. And, I am convinced, more and more of them will.

NOTES

1. Beverly Benner Cassara, ed., *American Women: The Changing Image* (Boston: Beacon Press, 1962). All but one of the contributors to this book were critical of women, but none so seriously as Margaret Mead, who said the scene did not make "a very pretty picture. . . . Why have we returned, for all our great advances in technology, to the Stone Age arrangement in which women's main ambition is to acquire and hold a mate, to produce or adopt children who are to be the exclusive delight and concern of a single married pair? . . . Woman has returned, each to her separate cave, waiting anxiously for her separate mate and

children to return, guarding her mate jealously against other women, almost totally unaware of any life outside her door. The woman who does not marry is frowned upon and discriminated against, given neither status nor honor. . . . Interest in any kind of work which might take precedence over the desire to have a family is discouraged; girls are admonished to study typing rather than mathematics. . . ." (p. xii). The following year Betty Friedan was to document these charges in greater detail. Against this background, the women in the present study look pretty good.

2. Ravenna Helson, "The Changing Image of the Career Woman," *Journal of Social Issues*, Vol. 28, 1972, pp. 33-46.

3. Paul C. Glick and Arthur J. Norton, "Perspectives on the Recent Upturn in Divorce and Remarriage," *Demography*, Vol. 10, August, 1973, pp. 301-314.

4. Kristin Carol Luker, *Patterns of Pregnancy: Towards a Theory of Contraceptive Risk Taking*, (Dissertation, Yale University, 1974), pp. 184-185.

5. The young women in the present study, with their desire for three children, belonged demographically in a transitional period. The desired number of children has fluctuated between 2 and 4; it had been high in the era of the feminine mystique, it is low now.

6. Ravenna Helson, *loc. cit.*, p. 44.

7. Robert Hefner, Virginia Davis Nordin, Meda Rebecca, and Barbara Oleshansky, University of Michigan Technical Proposal to National Institute of Education, Contract NIE-C-74-0144, May, 1974.

8. Jessie Bernard and Engin Holmstrom, "Sex-Role Transcenders and Sex-Role Transcendence," in Jessie Bernard, *Women, Wives, Mothers: Values and Options* (Chicago: Aldine, 1975)

9. If converts and shifters—both of whom as seniors had high Life Style Index scores—are added to the careerists, over half of the women in the present study were, to one degree or another, career oriented.

CAREERS AND CONTINGENCIES

Introduction

When we began studying college women, we were armed with a number of social-psychological studies about the career plans of college women. These were usually surveys done at one point in time and place. The findings were seemingly unrelated, confusing at best and contradictory at worst. We capitalized on the insights they presented and on the funds available to study a group of women throughout their college years, beginning when they began as freshmen and tracing the unfolding of their career plans until they were graduating seniors. Such a strategy of following the evolution of choices and changes is seldom possible, and we undertook the task with relish. The senior author began the research in 1964 and was joined two years later by the junior author, whose Ph.D. dissertation in 1968 was based on this research.

We could not anticipate the tiny sparks of feminist rebellion that sputtered in the late sixties and were fanned into open flames in the early seventies. While we were busy collecting data about life-style plans, other groups were challenging the validity of any quasi-traditional way of life for women.

So, a few short years later, one might well ask, "Why are you writing a book based primarily on a study that was completed in pre-liberation days? How can anything you have to say be relevant to today's woman? Hasn't the feminist movement changed everything?"

As scholars and activists we must unfortunately reply that while the new feminism has certainly raised every woman's consciousness, it has by no means altered the life style of even a minority of women. Today, young and mature women alike are confronted with the same basic issues they faced yesterday, last year and for decades before. What were previously essentially private struggles—whether to bear an unwanted child, how to get or retain credit when one's marital status changes, how to achieve a viable relationship with a man—are now simply more public ones.

The new feminism advocated offering women a wide variety of choices, but it has not yet drastically altered the basic dilemmas women face in making and implementing those choices. The women we studied show how necessary the Women's Liberation Movement is. There is a tension between children and career that is strong and real. There are time and energy constraints: "It's just plain hard to work, play, and rear a family." College women sense this and express the juggling process. They are the jugglers of gender—trying to incorporate expectations of procreation and domesticity along with expectations of greatness and satisfaction.

While new life styles and small families ease the burdens a bit, these changes are not radical enough to relieve the woman's problem. She struggles with ambivalence, and she plays with the choices because she has to juggle several *major* roles.

We wrote this book partly to tell this story—the story of the women whom we studied. But we also wrote this book to underline the fact that the problem will not go away. We are pessimistic despite all the current talk, hopes and even the glowing statistics about women's improved status. The increased enrollment of women in medical schools will not mitigate the trials of being all things to all people—to husband, children, boss and to society.

We welcome, indeed, the hopeful signs. But we show the despairing signs because they are loud and strong. The women we studied reveal the dilemmas. And daily more evidence accumulates to fuel our pessimism. The Women's Liberation Movement alone cannot bring progress. Only national policies affecting women can bring women to full access to careers and high achievement.

This book is about some women who, despite having gone to college in the dark ages of the late sixties, did indeed perceive a number of options and wrestled with their freedom to choose. Among the many influences that affect women, the most potent are people. Parents, teachers, counselors and educators may discover this material is relevant to their own decision-making.

By presenting the choices the women made, and the ones they left open, the factors they consciously used in shaping their plans and the forces that apparently caught them unaware, we have provided a solid background of base-line data against which new generations of students may be compared. The topics covered here cross several specialized fields including the status of women, the sociology of work, occupational aspirations, adult socialization, role theory and the impact of colleges on their students. These are topics that should interest social scientists from several disciplines: sociology, psychology, social psychology, anthropology and education.

Finally, of course, this book is addressed to today's students, both male and female, who, as the old stereotypes diminish, find themselves participating more and more as partners in common undertakings.

1   Education, Work and Women's Lives

This is a book about college women. In a society as affluent and open as ours, why should it be necessary to look at women as a separate category of persons? Women and men are thought to be equal under the law. Surely opportunities for work, education and general participation in family and society must be the same for both. Alas, these common assumptions are largely untrue. Women in America at all social levels have lower status, fewer opportunities and lesser achievements than men. It is astounding that even among college-educated women, the most educated and affluent women in America—and in the world—the problem of achieving full equality of opportunity persists.

Who is the villain of the piece? Ironically, no single villain exists. It is tragicomical that both men and women perpetuate vestigial traditional ways of thinking about gender. Parents raise their daughters to conform to the old molds. Teachers and counselors direct their pupils into paths of forty years ago. Most girls grow up accepting their places in life with a ceiling on opportunities and stop signs at higher educational and employment levels.

All around us in these activist times there is protest against inequality, against subtle forms of discrimination of all kinds. But shouting slogans does not liberate minority groups. It is necessary to study and understand the mechanisms and the contexts by which minority status is perpetuated. The college context theoretically offers the mechanisms for surmounting such minority status—the social limitations of gender. Probably in no other arena do women and men have so equal an opportunity to learn, develop, change, and explore. It is here that middle-class youth are launched into a wider society. It is here that aspiring lower-class children can climb into a more comfortable life. It is here that youth must make some choices and decisions for life. And it is here that choices of values, field, friends and a mate will occur, producing consequences that will last a lifetime.

As the last stage in development before adulthood, the college years should be the formative years. This is when youth are exposed to new learning, skills and ideas. No matter how unique any specific school may be, colleges share the aim of trying to make an impact on those who sojourn there. College education is not only preparation *for* life, it is also a forum for tasting *of* life. In both respects, college provides a special environment for persons between about eighteen and twenty-one years old, an environment in which to sample and study, to explore themselves and to discover the world, to choose work and formulate goals.

There is a strong evidence that colleges do affect and shape their students. They do so in both short-term and long-term ways. Over four years students generally become more liberal in political and social values and they become more mature in personality. Well into later life, college graduates show the fruits of higher education: their income is higher, they have professional-level jobs, they do community and volunteer work, they live in the life styles of the upper social strata. In these tangible ways they manifest dramatic advantages over the less educated. So these are indeed formative years for all students—women and men alike. But higher education can have a quite different meaning for women than for men, especially in the realm of careers.

Throughout the ages, women have worried about their

familial responsibilities, their centrality to others and their dependence on men. Educated women in America have wrestled with their intellectuality and rationalized the lack of opportunity to express it. In 1802, the nineteen-year-old Eliza Southgate Bowne, daughter of an upper-class New England family, wrote these words to her cousin:

> I have often thought what profession I should choose were I a man. The *law* would be my choice. When I might hope to arrive at an eminence which would be gratifying to my feelings. I should then hope to be a public character, respected and admired. To be an eloquent speaker would be the delight of my heart. I thank Heaven I was *born* a woman. I have now only patiently to wait till some clever fellow shall take a fancy to me and place me in a situation, I am determined to make the best of it, let it be what it will. We ladies, you know, possess that "sweet pliability of temper." But remember, I desire to be thankful I am not a man. I should not be content with moderate abilities—nay, I should not be content with mediocrity in anything, but as a woman I am equal to the generality of my sex, and I do not feel that great desire of fame I think I should if I was a man. (Eliza Southgate Bowne, 1888.)

These feelings and thoughts have not disappeared. Consider a young woman from an upper-class Pennsylvania family. An outstanding student all through high school and college, she majored in English and graduated with distinction in 1968. During the senior year, she said:

> I want to be active intellectually until my dying day, but even more than that I want to love a man, bear him children and make a home for my family. Hopefully, I can combine the two aspects of my womanhood—my biological with my intellectual destiny. I'm willing to set aside my intellectual goals for a number of years in order to begin the family since I strongly believe a mother should be with her children when they're very young. I guess my biological and traditional ideas of woman's role (*my* role) come first temporarily. On the other hand, ultimately, I really need to use my mind and I would be terribly resentful if I couldn't work eventually.

While much has changed in the 165 years between these two lives, the confusion and ambivalence about role choices remain. Both women hesitate to depart from what a woman's life should be. For Eliza Bowne it is a matter of making the "best of it" with a husband who chooses her. With the contemporary college girl, it is the priority of biological and traditional ideas of "woman's role." The similarity between two same-sex souls separated by eight generations stands out. Yet today's woman *can* become the lawyer Eliza could only fantasy about. And she *may* achieve the eminence Eliza dared to dream of. What we reveal throughout this book is that the paths to career for a woman are muddy and unclear, navigable but hazardous. The mere fact that she has choices to make poses a heavy burden. Occupational choice is only one element in a constellation of decisions about family, leisure and work. She need not decide to commit herself to work as a focal element in her life. She may remain a housewife or take on non-paying "work" or cultivate hobbies and interests. Or she may try to fit work in with all of her other life involvements.

The woman with professional career ambition faces three sources of constraints: those stemming from the professional world, those from her family, and those from the woman herself (Bailyn, 1973). Thus, an educated woman, despite her membership in the higher social strata, has to contend with realms of responsibility usually held by women in general. Even if she works, her involvements include home and family. Much as in earlier periods, the contemporary woman tries to juggle these involvements and responsibilities. In what follows, we show that while great progress has occurred for women, these barriers to women's achievement remain.

Women in the Labor Force

American women for many years worked side by side with their men on the farms and ranches of the frontier. Even after the rural population declined and town populations increased, households were close to being self-sufficient. Women were heavily involved in gardening, canning, pickling and preserving foods, making clothing, and preparing food from start to finish. Their labor has been characterized as having more usevalue than exchange value (Benston, 1972), yet many women did sell their products or services without being counted as employed (Smuts, 1960). Especially among the working classes, women supplemented the family's meager income by taking in boarders, sewing, doing laundry, and selling bread and other foodstuffs. They frequently assumed this piecework on top of crushing domestic burdens. Even middle-class women who had servants or hired immigrant girls to help were busy supervising and participating in all but the heaviest cleaning work.

Although the character of household work changed, it is important to recognize that the single major factor drawing women out of the home and into the labor force was a substantial alteration in the organization of the labor force itself; it was only secondarily a decline in the amount of labor married women perform at home.

At the turn of the century, one out of six women worked. At that time, the typical woman counted as employed by the Census Bureau was young, single and had opportunities in roughly three areas—teaching, domestic work for another family, or in one of the newly opened establishments where cloth or clothing was manufactured. Seven decades later, nearly one out of two women work, and the typical woman is middle-aged, married and employed as a secretarial, clerical or service worker.

This elliptical description indicates that a revolution has occurred in women's lives. Women's longer lifespan, their increased control over reproduction, and the concentration of child-bearing and child-rearing into an earlier and shorter segment of the life cycle are major factors accounting for such a revolution. Certainly all these events increased the amount of paid labor that women supply.

The character of work itself has changed. Originally primary activities, producing or extracting substances, were central. Unlike in England, women in America were never heavily involved in mining. They did, however, participate extensively in farming. The Industrial Revolution came late to this country. But when it did, and secondary activities turning raw materials into finished goods became dominant, women were quickly hired. They were especially used in the textile and clothing industry, as this represented an extension of the sewing, spinning and weaving they had already learned at home. Women were thought to be especially good at performing monotonous, repetitive tasks; they presumably had manual dexterity and a patience for routine.

The present surging demand for services means that many tasks formerly performed at home or done without are now done outside the home. Many more women are now paid for preserving or preparing food, for making or caring for clothing. Other services that even relatively low-income Americans can afford include entertainment and health and dental care. So women are drawn to work in laundry and dry-cleaning establishments, stores, restaurants, beauty shops, recreational facilities, doctor's offices and hospitals.

By 1956 there were more white-collar workers than blue-collar workers. This is largely due to the addition of female workers to the labor force and to the managerial revolution. As each new executive position opens, several new secretarial positions are created. A paper revolution has occurred—witness the veritable army of typists and clerical workers employed in business, in industry and government. While most clerical workers are young and many are single, increasing numbers of married women enter the labor force, attracted by the same economic forces:

> The industrial revolution and the changeover from a rural to an urban society, the campaign for women's rights, the work experience gained by millions of women during the war when there was a shortage of male workers, the shift away from physical and manual labor to lighter work in the factories, the

growth in white-collar jobs, and a rate of economic growth sufficient to generate an increasing number of jobs have all contributed to our almost matter-of-course acceptance of the presence of women in the labor force. (Perrella, 1968.)

The Limits of Women's Employment

Despite all these changes, women have not spread out in the labor force to assume jobs in all sectors. By 1970, women comprised 38 percent of all workers, yet in many of the more than four hundred job categories women were almost totally absent. Nearly two-thirds of female professionals are teachers, nurses, librarians and dieticians, occupations in which females predominate. While female enrollment in law schools and medical schools increased between 1960 and 1970, women are still only 5 percent of the lawyers, 9 percent of the physicians, 4 percent of the architects, 2 percent of the engineers, 3 percent of the dentists, 3 percent of the clergymen and 6 percent of the veterinarians. But they are 71 percent of the elementary and secondary school teachers, 94 percent of the nurses, dieticians and therapists, 79 percent of librarians and 70 percent of health technologists (U.S. Bureau of the Census, 1973). In short, over 80 percent of female professional and technical workers are in five occupations, each of which is overwhelmingly a female field.

Women are overconcentrated in the lower paying, lower status jobs, and underrepresented in the higher paying, higher status jobs. Women are much more concentrated into a limited list of occupations than men. Half of women workers are in only 21 occupations. It requires 65 of the largest occupations to encompass half of the male labor force.

The sex-segregation of the labor force has persisted for a long time. Occupations such as dressmaker, milliner, private household worker, nurse, hospital attendant, library attendant, librarian, telephone operator, teacher, stenographer, typist, and a host of operatives in paper, box and textile factories that were predominantly female in 1900 were still predominantly female in 1960. "During the 1900-1960 period, between 60 and 73 percent of the female labor force were in occupations where the majority of workers were women, and between 30 and 48 percent were in occupations which were *80 percent or more female*" (Oppenheimer, 1970, p. 70). Commenting on the fact that women accounted for 65 percent of the increase in the number of workers between 1950 and 1960, Rossi (1965) points out that a few occupations actually changed from being predominantly masculine to being feminine fields. These include bank tellers, peddlers and hucksters, and teachers in adult education, technical and private schools. There was no such dramatic increase at the upper reaches of the occupational structure. Among professional and technical workers women represented only 26 percent of the increase during the 1950s (Rossi, 1965). And:

> The number of occupations in which 100,000 or more women were employed increased between 1950 and [1970] by the addition of seven occupations—babysitter, charwoman and cleaner, counter and fountain worker, file clerk, housekeeper (apart from private household), stewardess, musician and music teacher, and receptionist—hardly impressive additions when one bears in mind the increased educational attainment of women during this period. (Suelzle, 1970, p. 52.)

If women have not radically altered their overall position in the labor force, is it true that they have entered the labor force in revolutionary numbers? The most dramatic increases in labor-force participation rates occurred since World War II. It is especially pertinent to focus on the time period from 1950 to 1970, as the work experience of the mothers of today's college youth is encompassed by these dates. In 1940, women were 24 percent of the labor force; by 1960 the number of working women had gradually increased until they were 33 percent of the labor force. The term "gradually increased" is appropriate, as the percent of women who work increased by approximately one half of 1 percent per year.

The figures for non-white females are also higher but lack the same rate of increase: 45.6 percent were working in 1948 compared with 49.8 percent in 1969 (Ferriss, 1971).

The figures for all women conceal startling differences in labor-force participation among age and marital status categories. Single, never-married women have work rates nearly identical to that of men. For example, among women 24-34 years old, 82.4 percent were in the labor force in 1969 compared to 87.8 percent of men. The work rates of single women remained constantly high over the 1950-1970 period. Married women are much less inclined to be employed. In 1959, 30.1 percent of married women were employed; by 1969 the figure increased to 39.5. Widowed, divorced or separated women work somewhat more often than married women do (Ferriss, 1971, pp. 371-372).

Since unmarried women were already nearly fully employed, the demand for workers was met by an increase in married women workers, particularly those who were over 40 years of age and who had no small children at home. After 1960 there were also substantial increases in the percentage of mothers with children under the age of six who worked. In the 1940s, less than one in ten of these women worked; now one in four do. Whether this trend will continue and more mothers with preschool children will enter the labor force depends heavily upon an increased demand for women workers and probably upon an increase in the availability of child-care facilities (Huber, 1973).

Women follow a pattern of cycling their employment to fit family needs. Thus women are rarely fully employed. Only 58 percent of women worked the full year in 1969, compared to 80 percent of men (U.S. Bureau of the Census, 1973a). The number of part-time workers reached 13.2 million in 1972, or 16 percent of total employment, and most of this was voluntary—four fifths of the part-time work force, mainly adult women and teen-agers, did not wish full-time jobs (Manpower Report, 1974). The modal pattern involves working until the arrival of the first child and then

resuming employment once children are at least in grade
school or high school. But part-year and part-time work
facilitate women's adaptation to both family and employment. Women thus show that they are still willing to accept
the "costs of motherhood" (Bernard, 1973).

When queried about their reasons for working, most
married women give a financial reason. They say they work
in order to purchase large consumer items such as furniture
or cars, to provide for their children's education, or simply to
supplement their husband's income (Sweet, 1973). Financial
need is a very apt description of their motivation, since a
disproportionately large share of the female labor force—over
two thirds—consists of single women, married women whose
husbands are not working, and married women whose
husbands earn less than $5,000 per year. "Financial neces-
sity" is not only an accurate indicator of the forces that
impel women to work, it is also a socially acceptable answer.
In this way women interpret their work as a service and
support for their family; they define their labor as part of
their maternal or wifely duties. Very few women work
because they want to do so or define work as a career that
precedes their family duties in importance.

It is ironic that women must work for money when their
rate of remuneration has remained consistently low. Full-
time, year-round women workers earn less than 60 percent of
the amount men do, and women's earnings (as a percent of
men's) have been declining at least since 1957. In 1970, the
median income for white male workers was $9373; for black
males it was $6598. On the distaff side, fully employed white
women earned $5490. Black women received the least of all,
only $4674, or exactly 49.9 percent of the amount white
males received.

Why are women's earnings so low? The stock answer to this
query is that women work in lower paying jobs and
industries; they are rarely unionized; they quit jobs frequently and fail to build up career experience. But these
phenomena do not in themselves account for all of the

sizeable income gap between men and women. A 1969 survey found that the average difference between men's and women's total compensation was $5000. Consideration of the number of hours worked, education, percent in unions, and the seniority of men accounted for only about half of the income difference, so there was a remaining, unexplained income gap of $2550 (Cohen, 1971).

While some researchers have observed large and puzzling income gaps between men and women, many are unwilling to attribute these differences to discrimination against women. In a study using 1970 census data on occupation, age, region and education, Almquist (1973) finds that probably a large portion of the unexplained income difference between white males and females is due to discrimination against women. In their study of university faculty, Gordon et. al. (1974) reach the same conclusion.

It is not clear what mechanisms are used to discriminate against women. Analytically one might distinguish between "antecedent" and "current wage" discrimination. Antecedent discrimination includes all those conditions that occur prior to receiving a paycheck that are discriminatory in character; for example, the fact that women's college scholarships and loans are lower than men's, the semi-formal quotas that operate to prevent women from entering professional schools, or the refusal to hire women in higher level positions. Current wage discrimination refers to paying women who have the same qualifications less than men are paid. Put simply, current wage discrimination is unequal pay for equal work (Almquist, 1973).

The existence of two separate labor markets in this country is a major factor keeping women's earnings low. Companies do not want to hire a secretary; they specifically want a female secretary. They do not seek persons for executive positions; they seek male executives (Oppenheimer, 1970). The market for male labor is simply more lucrative than the market for female labor. Recently lawyers who were filing sex and minority group discrimination charges against

American Telephone and Telegraph argued that when companies sex-label jobs and pay one group less, it comprises discrimination. They were able to make the charges stick. AT&T was ordered to pay women $15 million in back wages, the largest back-pay settlement in history. AT&T is the single biggest employer of women in this country. Women had long worked for "Ma Bell" as clerical employees and telephone operators, but they had not been hired as lineman, switchmen, installers, or repairmen—considerably higher paying jobs. "One expert for the EEOC estimated that 'women's' wage scale cost female workers $500 million annually" (Wohl, 1973, p. 58).

Besides employers' unwillingness to hire women in certain jobs, there is a reluctance to promote women when supervisory and higher level positions become available. When Women's Equity Action League investigated the banks of Dallas they found plenty of women employed as tellers, but virtually none were loan officers, a step up that males hired as tellers were almost universally likely to take. These items support the impression that Suter and Miller (1973) gained from survey data on income—women are simply unable to convert their educational and occupational attainments into income at the same high rate men do.

Women in the Home

If lack of opportunities for important jobs and economic discrimination prevail in the workplace, still other powerful forces operate to prevent American women from seeking careers. These cluster around the duties and responsibilities associated with domestic life. Every girl is socialized to want to marry and rear children. The socialization and training must be strong in order to insure that the society will not die out biologically and that *someone* will continue to perform very necessary tasks in the home. Yet once in the role many women find it confining.

It is instructive to consider housewifery, including the care of children, as an occupation. It is a very peculiar one. First, it is the only role with no qualifications other than sex. No occupation is so open to all comers, no occupation includes persons with such a wide range of ability levels. From genius to moron, all women, it is assumed, are qualified to perform the role. Second, in most occupations some service is performed or some good produced, and in one way or another the worker sees a product. The housewife sees her work consumed, the meals get eaten, the laundry and dishes must be done again and again. No wonder women find the household tasks that produce a lasting result, such as sewing and decorating, most satisfying. Third, most occupations require a fairly limited number of specific activities, which are to some degree integrated with each other. Not so for the housewife role. It involves diverse activities, ranging from boringly repetitive or menial tasks to enormously complicated ones. The contemporary middle-class housewife is expected and expects to be cook, dishwasher, child-care expert, nurse, domestic engineer, chief purchasing agent, maid, family accountant, den-mother, P.T.A. member, seamstress, gardener, and hostess—a rather dizzying array.

When the Chase Manhattan Bank added up the amount it would cost to replace that portion of the typical homemaker's chores that can be hired out, the total bill for a week's work came to $257.53 (Sherr and Kazickas, 1973). Yet unlike other jobs, housewifery does not command a paycheck nor are there contractual arrangements, fringe benefits, or social security. There are no specifications for hours to be worked and no days off. Payments are indirect in the form of support or maybe an allowance; at any rate, the housewife can expect no promotions and no raise in pay. In fact Caplow (1954) argues that the rewards a housewife receives are in inverse proportion to the effort demanded of her. This can be demonstrated in two ways. When the children are small she is at her busiest and the family income is at its lowest ebb. The lower the family income, the fewer labor-saving devices, the less household help and the fewer prepared products or services the family can afford.

Another set of job requirements stems from the number, ages and special needs of the children. Of course the definition of how much care a child requires varies from family to family. Yet all children pose at least some work for the woman, even if she does not answer their every beck and call. In other occupations, action is usually initiated for the worker by a superior. Beyond the minimum expectations of the husband, and the tasks imposed by children, there are few clear-cut standards for the woman.

The housewife does have a great deal of discretion in performing her work. She can decide the order in which she takes up various tasks and the amount of time she spends on them. In this respect she acts more like an independent professional than a constantly supervised factory employee. But such freedom carries with it an enormous burden. With no normative standards against which to weigh herself, she can never know whether her overall performance is outstanding or just adequate. For many educated women a kind of domestic anomie sets in. As a consequence, the woman may plunge into an upward spiral of cleaning, cooking, entertaining. With no one to compete against except herself, she engages in repetitive activity as if to prove that she is really capable. Part of the frenzy may be due to the fact that the housewife receives little coherent feedback about her performance. Initially husband or children may compliment her on an outstanding meal or for some special service she performs, but then they tend to take these for granted and few rewards are forthcoming until she again upgrades her performance.

Among the many alternatives that occurred in the housewife-mother role between the turn of the century and the present time, two trends are noteworthy: the increasing isolation of the household and consequently the wife, and the increasing psychological nature of the duties the wife performs. In 1900, an urban household was not considered middle class unless there were one or (usually) more servants. There were more children, and their age range was greater. The home was located fairly close to the husband's place of work; he spent more time there, often coming home for lunch. The household was likely to bear some resemblance to an extended family with an aunt, grandmother or cousin among the family members. Today's household usually includes only the husband, wife and children. Grandparents live alone or in the ubiquitous "rest home." Families live in the suburbs, husbands work in the city. Coming home for lunch is a rare event—if it happens at all. There are fewer children per household and, because they participate in many organized activities, they are at home less. Finally, except for an occasional cleaning lady or drop-in baby-sitter, the modern middle-class household is virtually servantless. The contemporary homemaker rarely has another adult woman around in whom she may confide or with whom she may discuss events. Of course, today's homemaker can and does decrease her isolation by participating in clubs and community activities, but typically these meetings are held outside the home. Thus, even for active leisure pursuits, the woman waits until her children are all of school age (Angrist, 1967).

Women are more likely to define themselves as mothers or homemakers rather than housewives. This may stem from the extreme degradation associated with domestic work or because of the greater virtue ascribed to raising children. There are several physical tasks associated with caring for a baby, but as the child grows older the tasks become more psychological in nature. Mothering a child amounts to an arena of activity where there are very few clear benchmarks against which to judge one's success or failure. Children's school performance may be the only regular indicator but this is by no means unambiguous.

With the growth in popularity of Freudian psychology and the appearance of the feminine mystique (Friedan, 1963) in the 1950s, American women began to define successful motherhood as their major goal in life. At the same time magazines began to popularize psychological literature deal-ing with such topics as marital conflict and child-rearing. Whether a woman has been to college or not, she unwittingly absorbs a large measure of this concern about her compe-tence as a mother and wife. If she works, she may feel guilty about tasks left undone at home and especially about the well-being of her children. After all, nearly all the experts, not just Dr. Spock, are unanimous in asserting that a preschool child can best be cared for by its own mother (Ainsworth, 1962).

A third change in homemaking is a decline in the sheer amount of physical work due to labor-saving devices. Have these aids substantially reduced the housewife's housework? One study found that the non-working woman averages 59 hours per week on housework (Walker, 1972). Such devices may merely permit a woman to do a better job of caring for her family. Instead of doing less she actually now has the time to do a wider variety of tasks (Oppenheimer, 1970). This notion harmonizes well with the view of housewifery presented earlier. A woman may not have to work so hard preparing formula any more, but now she expects to spend more time cuddling and playing with the baby. She does not wash laundry on a washboard but she and her family change clothes more often. She no longer has to bake bread, so she concentrates on gourmet dinners instead. With no standards to set an upper limit on what a woman should do, she merely uses the time gained to add other tasks.

External Barriers

It appears then that the housewife role offers two types of barriers that hinder women from selecting a career-oriented life style. One set of barriers originates in an economic structure making it difficult for a mother to compete successfully in the labor force and awkward to substitute readily for her labor at home (Lave and Angrist, 1974). That the external barriers exert a noticeable effect is evident especially for mothers. "An unemployment rate in March 1971 of 7.0 percent for married women (husbands present) with children, compared with a rate of 4.5 percent for those without children, indicates the difficulties in reconciling the needs of children with the needs of employers" (Hedges and Barnett, 1972, p. 11). For mothers of preschoolers the unemployment rate in that month was even higher at 10.2 percent. Hedges and Barnett (1972) report that in 1970, more than half of the 6.5 million women who ceased working in the previous 12 months mentioned home or school responsibilities as the reason.

The external barriers include the amount of housework deemed necessary and the difficulty of either shifting any of this burden to other family members or hiring household help. Women often allocate their time to carry out several tasks simultaneously. Individual women perform at different rates and hold different views about an acceptable quality and quantity of work. A Syracuse study reveals that wives who work 30 hours weekly or more still report spending 34 hours a week on household tasks. This lends support to the notion that women do not substitute paid work for housework when they take a job. They add the job and cope with the existing domestic responsibilities as best they can. Other evidence from the survey indicates that children's help was enlisted more often than that of the husband to assume part of the housework. These families have a rather traditional division of labor, with the husbands mainly making repairs and doing yard work (Walker, 1972).

Moreover there is a declining supply of domestic workers. In 1900, there was one private household worker for every 10 households; by 1960, there was one domestic for every 30 households (adapted from Oppenheimer, 1970). Between 1960 and 1970, the number of private household workers declined from 1.7 million to 1.1 million (U.S. Bureau of the Census, 1973a). This was at a time when the number of households increased and the number of women with families in the labor force hit an all-time high. Finally, even if household help is available, many women do not earn enough to hire such workers. A British study points out: "Because of decreased domestic help, the difficulties confronting a highly educated mother today may resemble those of a manual worker's wife more closely than those of professional women two or three generations ago" (Thompson and Finlayson, 1963).

The lack of suitable child-care arrangements remains a strong external barrier to women's careers. In 1970, 26 million children under the age of eighteen had working mothers. Nearly six million were less than six years old and hence were absolutely in need of care by an adult (Waldman and Gover, 1971). What strategies do parents have for arranging for the well-being of their children? One study of working women who had children under fourteen showed that 8 percent received no care at all. More than one fourth were cared for by the mother—parents worked alternate shifts or mothers worked only while children were in school. One can assume that these parents might like to have at least after-school care for their offspring. Nearly half of the children were cared for at home by someone other than the mother, a very expensive strategy. About one in five were cared for away from home, but less than 2 percent were in group-care facilities such as day-care centers or nursery schools (Low and Spindler, 1968).

Nuclear families usually cannot rely on grandparents and aunts for free and convenient child care as extended families used to. Increasingly, working mothers must take the child out of the home for child care and pay for such arrangements. While the expenditures for child care are relatively small, "the money . . . can be a drain on the woman's earnings, so that she has little left to show for her work" (Angrist and Lave, 1973). So far day-care centers and family day-care homes accommodate only about 10 percent of the children of working mothers. Thus, despite the growing need for out-of-home child-care facilities, mothers of preschoolers settle for a variety of child-minders, sometimes unreliable, but typically cheap.

In order to enter careers and compete successfully in their chosen fields, women need ways to surmount the barriers that prevail. While some barriers are external, others are internal—ways of behaving and believing learned in childhood and deeply ingrained through the growing-up process. In this chapter, we emphasized the external obstacles that women face when they contemplate and try to implement careers. Even for educated women who have the affluence of middle-class life, the barriers are solid both at home and in the world of work. At home, the woman's domestic responsibilities constrain her to commit boundless time and energy—husband and children come first. In turn, the work world demands at least a 40-hour week but offers low salary; it makes room in a "woman's field," but with low status. In the next chapter, we review the internal obstacles to careers, the "roots of women's ambivalence" (Rossi, 1967) in the socialization process. At first in the family, later in the schools, girls learn how to grow up female, how to learn a lot but seek a little, and how to equate pleasing others with developing one's self.

2 Career Commitment Is Hard to Learn

Despite family responsibilities, the lack of household and child-care help, and low remuneration, women work in even greater numbers. We can only infer from this that many women manage to circumvent these external barriers; they at least manage to hold jobs. But pursuit of a career usually requires long educational preparation, dedicated effort, long hours and an intense desire to achieve success. Because the external obstacles are buttressed by internal ones, career achievement becomes difficult indeed. For example, suppose the woman does locate a child-care center: then she begins to worry whether the facilities are adequate. Or suppose the husband does not object to his wife's working: still, she fears their relationship will deteriorate if she gets too involved in her job. These internal barriers thus rear their heads to constrain the woman's ambition.

The socialization process from childhood on works to limit women's career aspirations. It shapes a girl's personality, attitudes, beliefs and preferences, so that she wonders whether she can succeed in a career, she anticipates that certain professions and occupations are not receptive to women, and she dreads high achievement lest it spoil her life.

From the pink blanket in the nursery, through all the growing-up years, until the very end of her life, the treatment a woman receives and the experiences she undergoes are colored by the fact that she is female. There is some evidence that boys and girls differ at birth. Boy babies cry longer and louder, they are restless, wake more often and move around more. Initially the parents cuddle, touch and pay attention to boys more often than girls. Perhaps this is because they value boys more or it may simply be a response to boys' greater activity. At about six months, however, the situation reverses and girls receive more caresses and fondling while boys are talked to and sung to less. By the age of two, girls leave their toys and seek their mother's attention more often; by contrast, boys explore the house, seeking new areas of interest (Kagan, 1973). Michael Lewis reports the results of placing children in a room with toys, their mother, and eventually a fence that separates the mother and child:

> By the time they reach 13 months, boys venture significantly farther from their mothers, stay away from their mothers for longer periods of time, and look at and talk to their mothers less often than girls of the same age.
> Boys play more vigorously with toys, often banging them together, and play significantly more with non-toys (doorknobs, light switches and other room equipment). (Lewis, 1973, p. 48.)

While boys may have inborn tendencies to exhibit more autonomous and exploratory behavior, it is clear from simultaneous observations of parents that they encourage this in the socialization process. Our culture encourages independence in boys and dependence in girls. Males are expected to explore and master their world. Females are taught to stay close and to help their mothers. Both mothers and fathers seem motivated to foster these gender distinctions in young children (Hoffman, 1972; Lewis, 1973).

Since older children exhibit more gender-related behavior than younger children, and because American children manifest fewer sex differences than are observed in other societies, Chodorow (1971) concludes that sex differences are indeed cultural—that the behaviors are learned. She asserts that there are "no absolute personality differences between men and women, that many of the characteristics we normally classify as masculine or feminine tend to differentiate *both* the males and females in one culture from those in another, and in still other cultures to be the reverse of our expectations (Chodorow, 1971, p. 260)."

Nevertheless almost all researchers who have looked for sex differences in Americans have found them. It is well known that males and females score differently in nearly every personality trait psychologists deem important. The literature on sex differences is voluminous, but it has been well summarized by Bardwick and Douvan (1971). They ask, "What are big boys made of?" and to their own question reply unequivocally:

> Independence, aggression, competitiveness, leadership, task orientation, outward orientation, assertiveness, innovation, self-discipline, stoicism, activity, objectivity, analytic-mindedness, courage, unsentimentality, rationality, confidence and emotional control.
> What are big girls made of?
> Dependence, passivity, fragility, low pain tolerance, non-aggression, non-competitiveness, inner orientation, inter-personal orientation, empathy, sensitivity, nurturance, subjectivity, intuitiveness, yieldingness, receptivity, inability to risk emotional liability, supportiveness.
> (Bardwick and Douvan, 1971, p. 225.)

While these adjectives may sound like stereotypes for each sex, these are real characteristics that real people have. Rather than concluding that sex-related behaviors must be *either* genetic *or* environmental in origin, the experts agree that males and females are products of a complex interaction between both sets of factors (Bardwick, 1971; Maccoby, 1966). Even if we cannot or should not expect all women to develop analytic task-oriented cognitive styles nor aggressive unsentimental personality types, and if we cannot expect all men to become intuitive and sensitive cognitively nor yielding and supportive in personality, we can still expand the range of development from the constraints set by sex-role socialization.

The limits that socialization impresses on the woman involve a tendency both to underplay her own abilities and to value strongly family goals. These two elements are focal in the woman's contingency orientation.

A Contingency Approach

The research by Matina Horner underlines that "unfortunately femininity and competitive achievement continue in American society, even today to be viewed as two desirable but mutually exclusive ends." Women have a psychological barrier that is internalized early and "prevents them from actively seeking success . . ." (Horner (1972). Women not only learn consciously to avoid competing with men, they also learn to fear success unconsciously. Women college students were asked to write stories in response to the cue "After first-term finals, Anne finds herself at the top of her medical-school class." Many of the students responded with stories that expressed fear of social rejection, concern about normality or femininity, or simple denial of the reality of the cue. In some of the responses Anne suffers intense hostility from her classmates, loses her boyfriend, or drops out of medical school. Horner (1970) hypothesizes that women not only do not anticipate that rewards will follow upon successful achievement, but that in addition women fear punishment if they are successful in masculine areas.

What psychologists consider women's "fear of success," sociologists would prefer to call "role conflict." This perspective embodies the view that women not only learn "appropriate" feminine roles, including both attitudes and behavior, but that they also learn that family and career are incompatible. The language of role conflict has been popular because it appears to explain inconsistencies in attitudes as well as discrepancies between role conceptions on one hand and behavior on the other.

Unfortunately, the role conflict approach fails to apply consistently or clearly to either attitudes or behavior (Angrist, 1966). In a world of rapid social change, behavioral scientists are faced more with accounting for variation than for expecting total predictability in behavior. The research on women in general and our own work in particular lead us to view role performance as flexible, adaptive and accommodative rather than an all-or-nothing, either-or phenomenon.

What the role-conflict approach neglects is the potential most individuals have for playing many roles, for segregating the various and perhaps inconsistent roles they do enact, and for compartmentalizing attitudes in one area from viewpoints about other matters. If we approach social roles as static, assuming that expectations for behavior are near absolutes and that required role behaviors are exacting and concrete, then it is easy to slip into the trap of assuming that conflict between roles is inevitable. But for most roles a bundle of loosely intertwined attitudes is appropriate; expectations for sex-role performance in particular are elusive and vague. Nearly all roles have some stretch about them so that the individual is free to interpret, juggle, and actually perform in a variety of ways; it is more "role-making" than "role-taking" (Cf. Haga et. al., 1974).

But surely we must recognize that each individual normally plays a number of roles and in so doing the potential for conflict among the various roles looms large. It is true that no single role is ever isolated except conceptually—in reality, individuals relate to each other in terms of many criteria. One important device whereby people manage diverse multiple roles is by featuring one role above the other ones. Bates (1956) described this as a dominant role which, in appropriate contexts, supercedes latent roles. In this framework, age and sex are dominant roles subtly coloring how other roles are played. Thus father in the family is husband, sex partner, son-in-law, provider; influencing all of these is his dominant role of male. Women manage to be both mother and worker (and a good deal more) by choosing "feminine" fields of work and by working at times that do not interfere substantially with domestic requirements. An alternative mechanism for managing potentially conflicting roles is role segregation (Goffman, 1961), or scheduling role enactments so that their audiences are separated. Even when the actor is highly visible in a particular role, he or she typically shows "role distance" by exhibiting a certain objectivity, making light of the role, or allowing other peripheral roles to intrude on the situation. These are means for avoiding conflict or handling unavoidable conflict. Multiple role involvements allow the person to exercise perspective on any single role. Other things being equal, "the more roles in a person's behavior repertory, the 'better' his social adjustment" (Sarbin, 1954).

We believe that dealing with numerous and changing demands and performing a wide repertoire of roles should be recognized as normal. Instead of struggling to unravel the threads of women's role conflict, the research task should be to analyze the contingency orientation, the strategies women use for meshing different roles. The idea that people manage to juggle, avoid, manipulate, and interpret the scope of their behavior seems closer to reality than that individuals act in terms of a single-role blueprint at any given time or place. With regard to sex-role learning, it seems clear that it is not merely a process of increasing definition, knowledge, and specificity as the girl grows toward adulthood. Sex-role learning involves multiple conceptions of male and female roles, the recognition that there are various combinations of roles available to men and women in our society, and the realization that role constellations change as people move through different stages in the life cycle.

We offer the contingency orientation as a fresh approach to understanding women's role development. Instead of assuming that women are haunted by marriage-career conflict or paralyzed by their own feminine traits, we demonstrate that women are open to many possibilities and that they try to remain flexible and adaptable. They do not peg their plans on a single hook; instead they expect, realistically, to incorporate a number of roles into their adult lives. Such openness helps them cope with the many demands on their lives—marriage, child-rearing, work, community involvement, and the myriad other activities they expect to have.

Yet the flexibility also prevents single-minded pursuit of a career. As Komarovsky (1973a) points out, "sociological ambivalence" is a type of role strain that exerts a paralyzing influence on the individual. The same flexibility and openness can lead to indecision and hesitation to proceed.

How the Contingency Orientation Hinders Career Aspirations

Anne Roe (1963) noted that the characteristics of the successful, eminent scientist are high intellectual ability, independence, work persistence, an intense channeling of energy, and apartness from others. If girls are reared with an emphasis on sociability, charm, domesticity and popularity, these qualities adversely affect their chances for success in career pursuits. Indeed, most of the traits attributed to women and usually expected of them are the opposite of qualities that would enhance performance in a high-level career field. Thus, women are early losers in the competition to become eminent scientists.

Not only do women usually miss the chance in childhood to cultivate these qualities that would help them attain eminence, but even in late adolescence, when some encouragement to achieve may occur, they fail to exploit the opportunities. Among those who enter college, there is a hesitancy to proceed. Although overall aspirations for advanced education increase during college for both men and women, it appears to be more strongly accounted for by men (Astin, 1963). Women are less likely to choose fields requiring further education and to anticipate graduate study; this orientation is most characteristic of married or "attached" women and less so of single women.

Once in graduate school, the pattern seems to be perpetuated. Those women who do begin graduate school are less probable candidates for staying there than their male compatriots. Women more often than men consider withdrawing from graduate school, and they are more likely to perceive emotional stress as a deterrent to completing graduate work (Holmstrom and Holmstrom, 1974). In a follow-up study of rejected medical school applicants, Becker, Katasaky and Seidel (1973) find that women react differently from men to the rejection. The women tend to leave the hard sciences and enter fields with lower educational requirements (82 percent of the women rejectees became laboratory technicians!), and they more often than men rationalize that their rejection was "fair" even though they were as qualified as the men. Progressively smaller proportions of women achieve each degree level—while about half of bachelor's degrees are obtained by women, they comprise 40 percent of the masters, about 14 percent of the doctorates and only 6 percent of the professional degrees earned (U.S. Office of Education, 1971).

The consistency of this finding that young women have variant educational values and goals from young men is contrasted by the sex differential in academic performance. College women perform higher academically than men. The difference is not manifest at the level of top grades, but supports the impression that women get the B's while men get the C's (Davis, 1966; Lavin 1965). However, there is no indication that the sexes differ in general intelligence. Rather, qualitative differences in ability have been reported: starting at an early age, girls are typically better at languages, reading, writing and clerical skills, while boys excel in mathematical, mechanical and scientific aptitude (Hoffman, 1972; Maccoby, 1966). That girls get higher marks in school may result from their verbal and clerical advantages. Despite their higher academic achievement, women put less premium on getting good grades and as freshmen lose their grades orientation faster than men (Wallace, 1970). Thus the contingency orientation probably operative before college reemerges as women lower their vocational and postgraduate aspirations.

The uncertainty women have about themselves moves them to imagine that men hold low expectations for their achievement. Fichter (1972) reports that among Southern college graduates, both white and black women think that an advanced degree would lessen their chances of finding a husband. Thus some element of accepting traditional female roles continues to influence educated women's life plans.

Male Attitudes

How correct are women's perceptions of male attitudes toward working wives? Are women's beliefs that most men do not want them to participate in full-time careers justified? The answers to these questions can only be indirect, since sources of information are so varied. Public opinion pollsters frequently asked questions about women during the Depression years of the 1930s, but the number of questions on this topic dropped off drastically by the 1950s. That there have been startling changes in people's opinions about married women working is revealed by responses to a Gallup Poll question repeated after a 24-year interval. In 1945, only 18 percent said yes when asked, "Do you approve of a married woman earning money in business or industry if she has a husband capable of supporting her?" By 1969, 55 percent favored women working (Erskine, 1971). This shift of opinion, of course, accompanied the entrance of many women into the labor force over the same time period.

To ascertain the attitudes of contemporary males, it is relevant to consider recent studies of college men, a population that is probably more favorably disposed to career women than less educated groups and among whom college women are likely to secure a mate. In the fall of 1973, college freshmen were strongly in favor of the view that "women should have job equality"—88 percent of men and 96 percent of women said so; but in the same survey 41 percent of the men compared with 19 percent of the women endorsed the view that "married women's activities are best confined to the home" (Chronicle, 1974). So men are moving more slowly than women to accept the dedomestification of adult women.

Komarovsky (1973) found that a third of the men she interviewed in an Ivy League male college are troubled by a contradiction between the older norm of male intellectual superiority and the newer norm of intellectual companionship between the sexes. The remaining men can adjust in some way—by assuring themselves they are equal to their girl friends intellectually, by showing little interest in intellectual concerns, or by recognizing some weaknesses in their female friends that offset the girls' intellectual superiority. Only a few men consider their relationship completely equalitarian. The men were also queried about their attitudes toward their wives' future occupational roles. The traditionalists, who comprise 24 percent of the sample, want to marry women who would be sufficiently involved in domestic, civic, and cultural pursuits so that they would never seek outside jobs. The dominant response pattern includes half the men—those who hold a modified traditionalist position. They want a wife to work, withdraw from work for child-rearing, and return later. While the men vary in how these stages should be timed and in the amount of domestic help they would give their wives, most see no way to substitute for the mother's role in child-rearing during children's preschool years. The smallest group are those who take a feminist position. Seven percent of the total, they are the only ones willing to substantially change their roles in order to facilitate their wives' careers.

Komarovsky points out that allocating men's responses to a small number of categories covers up the tangled web of contradictory values and sentiments associated with these attitudes:

> In sum, the right of an able woman to a career of her choice, the admiration for women who measure up in terms of the dominant values of our society, the lure but also the threat that such women present, the low status attached to housewifery but the conviction that there is no substitute for the mother's care of young children, the deeply internalized norm of male occupational superiority pitted against the principle of equal opportunity irrespective of sex—these are some of the revealed inconsistencies. (Komarovsky, 1973, p. 881.)

In another study from a midwestern university, about two fifths of the males prefer that their future wife work until the arrival of children and then work no more unless it becomes absolutely necessary. Another two fifths prefer that she work until the birth of children, devote full time to family during the children's early years and then return to work as the children grow older. Less than 4 percent want a wife who would "work in the profession rather continuously after marriage, taking off only short periods of time when required by family matters" (McMillan, 1972, p. 9).

Almquist (1974) studied attitudes toward female employment among both male and female students at a southwestern university. Women were asked whether they wanted to be employed under each of a variety of circumstances, and men were asked whether they wanted their wives to work in each situation. There is a high degree of agreement between males and females. Less than 10 percent of either group want a wife to work when children are preschool age; half the males and two thirds of the females want the woman working when children are in school. The situations most conducive for the woman's employment are when a husband's salary is inadequate; before children are born; when the husband is in graduate school; or when the husband is unemployed. Nearly all are willing for a woman to be employed under these circumstances, suggesting strongly that both men and women define a woman's work as supplementary to the male's main task of breadwinning, rather than as a career in its own right. Overall, the women are only slightly more interested in working than the men are in having their wives work. The responses of the two sexes diverge only in one item: 37 percent of the females but 67 percent of the males want a wife to work if she can earn more money than the husband.

The results of these studies suggest two conclusions. First, no dominant orientation toward women's careers exists among men, except that many still reflect the prevalent American norm that prescribes personal care of young children by the mother. Parenthetically we note that this orientation is dysfunctional for the wife. If she has two children and pauses in her career pursuit until they are in school, she will lose a minimum of five to ten years. This self-imposed interruption nearly prohibits work in such fields as law, medicine and science, fields requiring years of advance preparation and continuous participation to keep up with developments. Women typically take time out to have children just when their male colleagues are finding a foothold on the occupational ladder, setting up a practice, or getting those first, important promotions. The second conclusion is that men are still far from strongly favoring women's involvement in careers.

Dual-Career Families

It is not surprising that males express ambivalence toward a career wife. If female career-role models are lacking for women, there are probably fewer models of men who combine career with deep involvement in family life and who make it possible for a wife to have her own career. Dual-career families are rare in America. From reports about those that do exist there appear to be two major patterns. In one, the wife essentially begins her career after the children are born. Perhaps she even waits until this time to acquire professional training. In these families, according to Poloma (1970), the husband and wife almost never establish equalitarian family roles; instead they have neo-traditional families where the wife retains ultimate responsibility for child care and hiring and supervising domestic help. The women's reasons for working seldom involve money; more likely motives are sheer enjoyment and personal fulfillment. They continue to see the family's social status as primarily determined by the husband's professional standing and to place his career concerns first. Moreover, unlike their husbands, the women adjust their work schedules and commitments over time to suit family exigencies.

In the second pattern, both spouses adapt their career development to each other's as well as to family demands. The spouses may marry young and go through training and early career stages together. Children are deferred, but after each childbirth, the wife quickly returns to work (Rapoport and Rapoport, 1971). The spouses have essentially shifted away from conventional sex roles, so that the husband is "family-oriented" and the wife is "career-integrated"–"both have added to their traditional concerns an emphasis on the realm most commonly associated with the other sex" (Bailyn, 1970, p. 102). In order for this pattern to succeed, the husband can value career achievement, but not too much. Instead of the wife as the key accommodator to his life style, the husband eases the constraints by accommodating to hers also (Bailyn, 1973).

Still other strategies include remaining child-free, or for the husband to interrupt *his* career during the early child-rearing stages. While all these options are growing, they continue to be rare and difficult to implement. What some call "revokability" continues to plague even those women who achieve high-status professions (Bailyn, 1964; Epstein, 1970). At each point in her ascent up the career ladder, potent forces pull the woman down or make her stand still. Little positive encouragement, much denigration and ambivalence are the rule. Thus, instead of seeing her career as a deliberate climb up a ladder, step-by-step, the woman hesitates; she constantly feels tempted to stop or retreat, to sink into home-bounded domesticity or to settle for less in her work. She may revoke what she has already attained in order to remain open to the hazards of family life.

College Women's Role Development

We have argued that there are strong forces that prevent women from achieving careers. These forces are not merely in the world of work, they are also embedded in women's own conceptions. Since university education is the key stepping-stone to high-level professions, it should socialize women both to aspire and to achieve such careers.

How much can college move women toward careers? While it would be incorrect to conclude that college has no influence on women's later life styles, neither is it clear what the precise effects are. In the broadest sense of life style as social class level, income and occupation, college-educated women, mainly via their spouses, differ predictably from the non-college-educated. But life style in terms of the relative priorities given to advanced education, marriage, family, leisure and work is far less predictable. Least definitive is the extent to which the adult woman's career pursuits can be foreseen from her career interests as a college student. While college education increases the likelihood that a married woman will seek gainful employment, it does not appear to point her inevitably toward a career. The contingencies in her adult life predominate and move her toward conventional role behavior even in her choice of an occupation.

When a woman enters college, she already manifests the sex-tied behaviors and values she learned earlier. She wants to be conventional and practical even in the choice of major field. She wants work presumed appropriate for a woman and which does not call for long-term preparation or involvement. On the whole, both women and men lose interest in scientific and engineering careers during the four years of college (Astin, 1972). Nevertheless, when the sexes are compared, women's preferences emerge in distinctive ways. While males are likely to enter the physical sciences, engineering, agriculture and business, females tend to pursue education, humanities, fine arts, social sciences and biology. During college, most of the initial field choices gain increasing favor. Women move more heavily than earlier into education, but defect from the social sciences at a high rate. Thus the fields that emerge as more feminine by senior year are education, humanities and the fine arts, while the initially masculine fields of engineering, sciences and business become more so (Davis, 1966). It is clear, then, that as undergraduates women choose predominantly female-dominated major fields.

The contingency orientation begins long before college— but how well developed is it, and how does college affect it? Do college women become more career-oriented during the four years? What distinguishes those who do aspire to careers from their more traditional classmates?

This book presents college women who were studied intensively over each of the four years to observe their attitudes, plans and aspirations for adult life, especially their career aspirations. A longitudinal study design makes possible a detailed view of their role development. If students are affected by college, presumably this transformation occurs between freshman year and graduation. So we studied more than the net effect of college. Our strategy was to look at the college years microscopically, one by one. The women comprised one class in one women's college, part of a larger coeducational university with a strong professional-vocational orientation. There were 188 freshmen women who began college together in 1964; of these, 58 percent or 109 were graduated together four years later.

These college women do not represent all college women.

They compose one small sample drawn from a particular school at a specific time. Strictly speaking, the study participants can only illuminate their own college experience and aspirations. Still, the possibility looms large that features of these women, even odd or minor ones, will be found among other contemporary college women.

This book encompasses eight years of thinking, talking and writing about the college women who participated in our study. In the pages that follow we try to synthesize, digest and describe what we have learned about these women. We try to reflect and interpret their experiences as the students conveyed them to us in lengthy interviews and on multiple pages of questionnaire. The yards of tape-recorded interviews and the pounds of questionnaire paper were supplemented by college records. All together, these comprise the raw data and this book itself is necessarily but a distillation of that data.

The aim of this book is to highlight and to explain the students' development as educated women—their impressions of what college is like each year, how their hopes and plans for after college develop, the way in which these ideas change and the forces that encourage or inhibit career plans. The students are presented both statistically from their question-naire answers and in depth through their own words as expressed in interviews. They emerge through their hopes and dreams, their frustrations and disillusionment, and their general outlook toward life's contingencies as seen from the promising yet hazy springtime windows of senior year.

We will consider the extent to which the college context illumines student life-style preferences. We show that women choose an occupation within the context of a whole constellation of roles as worker, wife, mother, woman—they do not simply choose a field of work, they elect a total life style. We also consider the continuing and often enriching influences of family, high-school and college experiences, of teachers, professors, boyfriends and girl friends. We will paint portraits of the career-oriented and non-career women showing the key features of their hopes and plans for adulthood. Finally, we will discuss the benefits and limitations of college education for women, emphasizing strategies that educators, counselors, parents and young women themselves can use to foster career interests.

The university at which this study took place has a special professional emphasis that stems from its technological institute origins in engineering and the sciences. But the emphasis pervades the entire school and strongly colors its reputation. The research then was framed in a particularly relevant setting, one that attracted work-oriented women more than other colleges and should have channeled their interests toward work, even careers, after college. And indeed as these women grew generally more interested in the world of work, they lost some of their conventional role conceptions by the end of the college period. But this is not the whole story. There are three elements that stand out: first is the contingency approach, which they brought to college and continue to use, juggling and weighing alternatives while avoiding any fixed career commitment; the second is the variation in role outlook within the class ranging from total career concern at one end to total absence of career interest at the other; and the third is the importance of mothers, teachers and peers as influences on career aspirations. As the findings unfold, it will become clear that most of the women expect to work at some time after college. But work is not the same as career; only some women become career-oriented during college, most lack career aspirations entirely and many lose such aspirations as they move through college. In this formative context, what is thought "suitable for a woman" predominates.

The reader must recognize that some issues raised by Women's Liberation were with us long before the movement. Generations of thoughtful women struggled with what it means to be a woman. This book will show that these same issues remain unresolved, and that they will stay to haunt women long after the Women's Liberation fire fades: the oscillation in making life plans, the obstacles in pursuing careers, the pressure to marry and have children, the uncertainty about goals and the ambivalence about achieving eminence. But this book will also show that there are conditions that nurture career aspirations and which can be feasibly implemented.

3 College Fosters Career Interests, But...

To understand the development of women's career aspirations, it seemed logical to study them in a context in which some students do show career interests. The research setting was a women's college within a private university that had achieved national eminence through its reputation in science and engineering. The institution has changed since the study. What was a technological institute became a university; what was a women's college is no more. Despite these changes, we believe there is a constancy about college students and about women so that the students whom we studied were not wholly unique.

The school was considered small, with a total enrollment of 4000 students, of whom 3000 were undergraduates. There were strong curricula in the fine arts and liberal arts, yet the school was defined primarily as a "technological institute," with a preponderantly male student body. A pronounced professional-technical emphasis emanated from the engineering and science fields and graduate programs, encompassing programs in music and art, and extending to the women's college as well. We expected both the larger university and the women's college to attract career-aspiring girls since avowed goals of the college were to cultivate women's interest in the work world and to channel specific career choices.

We studied students of one class in the women's college intensively during their college years. They were predominantly white, middle class and from the Northeastern states. They majored in English, history, economics, psychology, social science, biology, physics, chemistry and mathematics. The study class began with 188 freshmen, of whom 58 percent graduated together four years later. The findings in this book are based on the panel of 87 students (or 85 percent of the class) who went through college in phase *and* who provided complete questionnaire data all four years. Appendix 1, How the Study was Conducted, presents our research procedures in detail for readers who are interested in the setting, research design, data collection, reliability and validity of the data. In the next section we present only a few highlights of the research methods.

The Panel of Students

We utilized both questionnaire and interview responses from the 87 women who served as the four-wave panel for study. By using the answers of the same persons at different time points we systematically tracked how people actually change. The panel method (Wiggins, 1973) obviates the need for people to recall their previously held attitudes. While dispensing with the problem of hazy memories, the panel study also increases the probability that the researcher, through repeated questioning, will discover changes in viewpoint that the respondent herself does not even perceive.

In order to develop this detailed picture of the process by which college women develop their ideas about adult roles, we scrutinized their choices, preferences and plans for life after college. The college years were surveyed microscopically to chart the patterns of choice and change on several key aspects of post-college life, including intention to attend graduate school, decidedness of occupational choice, work preference, work motivation, willingness to pursue a career even during the child-rearing stages, and ideas about child care, marriage and the domestic division of labor. Each year, the answers students gave to specific questions were dichotomized as yes or no, favorable or unfavorable, decided or undecided, and the like. Each question yields four sets of two possible answers that can be diagrammed as a shifting process (Figure 3-1). We begin with the freshmen, who either said yes or no, and follow them through each subsequent answer as sophomores, juniors and seniors.

While two-wave panels are very common, especially in studies of voting behavior, four-wave panels are rare. Primarily because of the expense, they are seldom applied even in the plethora of studies of college students. The panel method used over four time periods provides rich information on how consistent or haphazard the students are and on the specific patterns and the timing of changes, as well as the directions such changes take.

The Search for a Life Plan

Have the four years of learning, exploring, searching and trying things—courses, professors, roommates, boyfriends, activities, majors, jobs—given women the formula, the rational plan, by which to proceed? Do college girls pursue one line of action single-mindedly, or do they adopt some other strategy? Do views of adult life acquire more consistency and directedness as students face leaving the embrace of the women's college to enter a new stage in the life cycle?

We find that the students generally change their outlook somewhat during the college years, but they move in both directions: some develop career interests and others relinquish them. Occasionally a coherent unified plan emerges for the after-college life:

Each woman must decide her role. For me, that of wife and mother is the most important thing in the world. I plan to work with mentally retarded children until my fiancé receives his Ph.D. in chemical engineering. At that time, I will terminate my vocation and become wife and mother full time. I can hardly wait.

More often, the search for a life plan intensifies with many unknowns and a desperation about how to combine family, children, and work:

> The first two or three years have just been going to classes and not thinking about myself, what I want to do. This year, naturally, I'm beginning to think: what am I going to do? And I really don't know, which sort of panics me. I am getting married and I have to get a job and I don't know what I want to do yet.

Some students face the end of four years with panic, others with relish. There can be a sense of accomplishment or an uncertainty fraught with anxiety. The last year of college calls for future plans, but few have made definitive decisions. How to articulate one's interests with life's opportunities, how to weave a meaningful whole from fragmented bits— these matters preoccupy the senior women. They seek to comprehend and tentatively to untangle the still untouched web of job-school-husband-children.

Education and Work Plans

Three aspects of the process by which the college-educated decide about the world of work are considered here: plans to go to graduate or professional school for further training, the decision to pursue a specific field of work, and the type of occupation selected. The study class is consistently high in favoring postgraduate education for themselves and quite inconsistent in picking an occupation, with their choices falling predominantly within women's professions.

When students were asked "How much education does a woman need nowadays," the majority answered "college graduation" and a tiny 16 percent said postgraduate training.

Even though the class devalues graduate training for women generally, their specific plans for themselves are quite another matter. They are initially strongly oriented toward graduate school and become increasingly committed to it. As freshmen, 56 percent say that they plan to continue their education after the baccalaureate. As they move through the college years, a growing portion of the class hopes to pursue graduate training. There is a sharp rise in the number of students aiming for advanced education after the start of junior year, so that 61 percent of the juniors and 76 percent of the seniors plan to continue. (Figure 3-1).

Just over a third of the class steadfastly sustain such plans each year. They seem to anticipate these aspirations and hold onto them throughout college. Only 16 percent of the students consistently shun graduate school plans all four years. As Figure 3-1 shows, the students who develop graduate school plans come from the 44 percent of the class who are either initially uncertain or not interested. Each year, from this segment, small numbers convert from having no further educational plans to formulating some.

The disciplines selected by the study class are very like the distribution of fields selected by a national sample of women college graduates (Women's Bureau, U.S. Department of Labor, 1966). Their choices are quite similar over the four years with seniors more often opting for English, language, journalism and professional fields than students at any other class level. All together, half of the seniors choose graduate training in social work, library science, education, literature and writing. An additional 7 percent plan professional study in medicine and law.

Since more students make graduate school plans each year, one can guess that they are responsive both to the school's orientation and to the larger social climate that stresses advanced training. At this women's college, about 15 to 20 percent of the students went to graduate school in the early 1960s. By the late 1960s the proportion had risen slightly to 23 percent. So these girls mirror the trend. Even so, it is not

Figure 1   Changes in Graduate School Plans

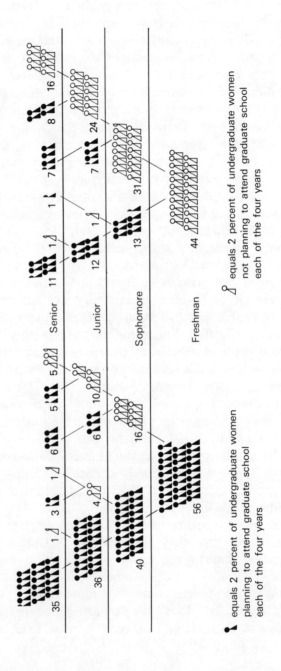

♪ equals 2 percent of undergraduate women
   not planning to attend graduate school
   each of the four years

● equals 2 percent of undergraduate women
   planning to attend graduate school
   each of the four years

obvious that all the graduate-school aspirants mean to continue on directly after college. Some girls were speaking about the future, hoping to enter graduate school after working for a year or two, or at an even vaguer later time when children are grown and they are ready to re-enter the labor force. Others intend graduate study not in the strict sense of working toward an advanced degree, but as recreational courses or certification for an occupation such as teaching. As the Katz (1969) study on Stanford women shows, while the rates of entry to graduate school may be high, the retention rates are dramatically lower. Not only do proportionately fewer women then men enter graduate school, they also are less likely to stay there. Still we must stress that the study class manifests very high interest in graduate training, and the pattern of changing is predominantly toward developing such plans rather than relinquishing them.

Choosing an occupation is a more difficult matter than thinking about graduate school, more hedged with uncertainty and doubt. On each administration of the questionnaire, we asked students, "As things look to you now, do you feel you have chosen a specific occupation or field of work you would like to enter after graduation from college?" If the answer was yes, they were asked to describe it as precisely as possible, to indicate how certain they were that they would actually pursue the occupation, and how easy or difficult it had been for them to choose. If the answer was no, they were asked, "What one occupation or field of work would you choose if you had to decide right now?" Only 38 percent of the freshmen, half of the sophomores and juniors, and 64 percent of the seniors feel decided about an occupation. This means that fully 36 percent of the seniors remain undecided about what occupation to pursue. Only 15 percent feel decided about work choices from the beginning to the very end of college. Similarly, 14 percent are undecided in each of the four years. As Figure 3-2 reveals,

Figure 2   Changes in Decision About Occupation

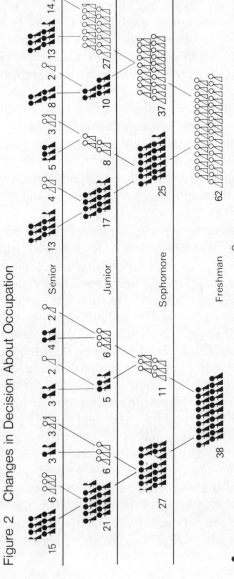

♪ equals 2 percent of undergraduate women who feel decided about occupation each of the four years

♀ equals 2 percent of undergraduate women who feel undecided about occupation each of the four years

the remainder oscillate between decision and indecision, knowing and not knowing.

Analysis of the actual occupations selected confirms the students' indecisiveness. Only four students maintain by senior year the same occupation they had as freshmen. Among the students who change their choices, some do so repeatedly. The picture improves somewhat when the certainty of choice is considered. Among freshmen, only 5 percent feel very certain they would actually follow their chosen occupation. In senior year one third feel very certain and another one third feel fairly certain that they would pursue the occupation they had selected. And some of the students who are undecided in the fall make more explicit plans by the time of the spring semester interviews. To look only at senior choices would obliterate the fact that most students had quite different intentions as freshmen than they held as seniors, and nearly all underwent times of indecision and floundering in the intervening years. The inescapable conclusion is that change rather than stability is the characteristic pattern from which few women escape.

What occupations do the women eventually settle on? Looking at their senior questionnaire responses shows that high-school teaching is the single occupation most frequently selected (Table 3-1); for these 24 percent, their fields cover the several majors—social science, history, English, business, home economics and mathematics. College teaching is chosen by 10 percent; mainly English or history majors. One in seven students plan research careers in such areas as psychology, chemistry, foods or biology. Law and social work are each chosen by three students.

Department store buyer is a popular choice among students who specialized in textiles and clothing or design and retailing. Eight students indicate buying as their preference, with others selecting merchandising or working in private dress shops. Five students from the foods and nutrition option in home economics plan to implement their

Table 3-1. Fields of Work Chosen by Seniors

Field	Percent
High-school Teacher	24
Department store buyer	14
Research	14
College teacher	10
Nutritionist, dietician	6
Lawyer	3
Social worker	3
All other occupations, including "don't know"	26
Total	100%

training by being a nutritionist or a dietician or by working in a food company.

The remaining choices are scattered among such diverse fields as interior design, personnel management, journalism, advertising and technical writing, counseling and clinical psychology. A very few students do not indicate a specific occupation. They simply specify a discipline such as economics, psychology or education. Only two students state flatly, "I don't know."

Considering the class as a whole, certainly the students will be joining the labor force in a variety of work contexts. They will work in government agencies, hospitals, pharmaceutical industries, universities, high schools, law firms, publishing houses, food companies, department stores and other retail outlets. Some will go immediately from graduation to work; others will be engaged in lengthy graduate programs with definite occupational goals in mind; another few are postponing specifying a particular occupation until they have completed graduate study.

It is noteworthy that few students are oriented toward positions as administrators or executives in business fields. Perhaps those interested in buying, personnel management or merchandising come closest. Similarly, few are selecting occupations in the clerical or sales categories. The majority—

over two thirds—of the choices fall within the professions; this is consistent throughout the four years.

Categorizing college women's occupational choices as professional or non-professional does not meaningfully divide the sample. A more interesting division emerges by ascertaining whether students prefer occupations that are traditionally feminine or whether they intend to crash the gender barriers by entering male preserves. We rated each girl's annual occupational preference according to its typicality for women. Typical occupations are those in which women comprise more than one third of the practitioners, since women constituted one third of the labor force in 1960. Examples of typical occupations are high-school teacher, dietician and social worker. Atypical occupations are those in which less than one third of the workers are women, such as mathematician, lawyer or business executive. In many of the occupations that are atypical for women, less than 10 percent of the workers are female. Note also that these male-dominated fields are the higher level professions and generally connote high social status.

Among the students, 18 percent choose typical and similarly 18 percent choose atypical fields at all four time periods. Thus somewhat over one third of the students do not change at all in this respect. Figure 3-3 illustrates that students more often pick male-dominated fields early in sophomore year than at any other stage. But this must be viewed as temporary, since several students leave their unconventional choices by junior year. In all, 21 percent defect to typical women's occupations between freshman and senior years, while 17 percent become converts to masculine fields. And 26 percent simply fluctuate, switching back and forth between atypical and typical occupations for women. In the end, high-school teacher is the most frequently chosen typical field while college professor is the most preferred of the atypical occupations. To the high interest in professional level work noted earlier, we must add this qualification: a majority of seniors opt for traditionally feminine fields.

Figure 3 Changes in Typicality of Occupation

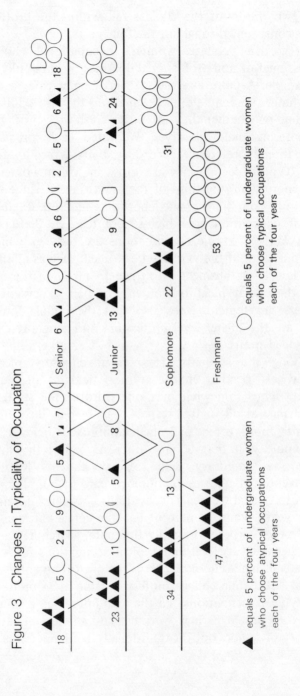

▲ equals 5 percent of undergraduate women
who choose atypical occupations
each of the four years

◯ equals 5 percent of undergraduate women
who choose typical occupations
each of the four years

Conceptions about Family

We turn next to women's ideas about marriage, family, and child care, areas that frequently provoke written commentaries from the students. These comments might be taken as a good-natured unwillingness to respond definitively to questionnaire items, or a desire to qualify and elaborate their answers. Just as certainly, however, they highlight the hesitancy to form commitments and the ambivalence surrounding their post-college lives.

There is small doubt of the desire for family life since nearly all students (96 percent) want to marry, and a smiliar proportion hope to have children, about three on the average. At first they do not want to rush into family life. About one-third of the freshmen say they would prefer to marry at ages 23 or 24, and most of the students want to wait until college graduation. Later the enthusiasm for deferred marriage wanes. There is a progressive drop in the proportions of sophomores, juniors and seniors who prefer to wait and marry after age 24. Very few students, only 9 percent, consistently think it a good idea to marry late, while 29 percent, all through college, firmly prefer to marry before age 24.

The growing desire to marry earlier partly reflects the fact that students become increasingly "attached" to a male:

> I noticed that my ideas have changed considerably about women's roles since I have considered marriage and the beginning of a family in the next year or so. Before I answered the questions hypothetically. Now they have more meaning.

By senior year, half the students are going steady, engaged or already married. Some can barely conceal their delight:

> I am pinned to the greatest guy; we are going to be married after we graduate . . . I love him and intend to be his wife above all else.

Only one or two students are unwilling to express a definite best age to marry, suggesting that decision must wait until the right man comes along:

> I honestly don't know. When I find a man I really love and want to marry, I'll notify you immediately!

Despite the growing urge to marry early, these women shift surprisingly in their ideas about family life. In general, they become less traditional in outlook toward relationships with husbands and children. We tapped their attitudes about domestic matters through a set of statements on Sex Role Ideology (Hoffman, 1963). Each statement describes a possible division of family responsibility between wife and husband, and for each, the students indicated how strongly they agree or disagree:

> Raising children is more a mother's job than a fathers.

> Except in special cases, the wife should do the cooking and housecleaning and the husband should provide the family with money.

> If the man is working to support the family, his wife has no right to expect him to work when he's home.

> A man who helps around the kitchen is doing more than should be expected.

> A man ought to feel free to relax when he gets home from work.

Total scores range between 1 and 25, with a higher score reflecting more traditional views and a lower score as more modern.

The seniors change their views considerably from the views they held as freshmen. Sixty-three percent score as traditional the first year compared with only 40 percent in the fourth year. Thus the students become generally more equalitarian about marriage. By senior year, 32 percent adopt a modern outlook and only eight percent shift to a traditional viewpoint. But nearly a third move back and forth between modern and traditional attitudes concerning appropriate husband-wife roles.

Among the class members, a wide range of opinions is evident. Few are as equalitarian as this married student:

> My husband and I plan to share as equally as we can in raising our children and living our lives. Right now we split the housework evenly with due respect to specialties. He can't sew and I can't use a saw. We both intend to work when we have children. He is willing to work part-time if our children need his attention and there is no excellent child care available, as will I.

Nor would very many consent to the other extreme:

> A woman who is married should do everything to please her husband and nothing that disagrees with him . . . within reason. She should love him very, very much and depend on him for affection, love and masculine guidance.

The dominant view if that the spheres of husband and wife overlap somewhat:

> Marriage is a two-way proposition, and the woman and man involved should share the responsibilities of maintaining the home and financial situation. One of the most important things a woman should understand is that the bills are not just the man's problem. Everything important to both parties should be discussed in detail before a final decision is made.

Where children are involved, the class also moves in a more liberated direction, favoring greater freedom for mothers of young children. As freshmen, 65 percent think that "a mother with children between the ages of one month and six years should personally care for them throughout the entire day." As seniors, only 39 percent strongly agree. The drop in this conviction is radical between sophomore and junior years. Yet it is important to recognize that a solid fifth of the class maintain this belief throughout college:

> A woman's first duty is to her husband and children . . . When her children are of preschool age, they are very dependent on her and she should be able to be there at all times. Once they are in school, their dependence on her decreases and she may (and probably should) widen her interests.

Other students fear that continuous care can be too confining, perhaps even damaging to the children:

> I certainly do not intend to be one of those women who wrap their whole lives up in their children and who feel useless with nothing left to do when they leave home. A frustrated mother is much worse for her child's development than a mother who is happy and satisfied working at a part-time job. Children can be made to feel loved and secure in many other ways than by having a doting mother around constantly.

Among the 62 percent of students who change their minds on this point, most shift within one end of the continuum from feeling very strongly to moderately strongly. Thus, overall the class emphasizes a mother's need to provide continuous care for her preschool children.

Combining Work and Family Life

Once college women begin to weigh the kinds of role combinations they may face, their ambivalence about work grows. More particularly, a solid segment of the class finds it impossible to put career above family. The dominant conception is that life plans revolve around one's family situation. Under some conditions, when children are very young, even financial need fails to push the woman into a career-salient mode. Under other conditions—having school age children or children who are grown up—work once again appears a likely pursuit. For most women, the desire to work is not a compelling motive that operates in all situations; rather it is tied to specific conditions.

We used several different questions to gauge the students'

career commitment. To measure work motivation we asked students how they feel about holding a job after marriage and graduation from college, and whether they thought they would work under specific conditions involving the number and ages of children and the adequacy of husband's salary (Eyde, 1963). Almost no girls say they would work when they have preschool children and the husband's salary is adequate. Several more want to work when they have preschool children, but only if the husband's salary is inadequate. Some students do not even anticipate this as a realistic possibility:

> My background has been above adequate financially, so I probably would not marry a man who cannot provide for a family.

By contrast nearly all would work when they have no children regardless of the husband's earnings or when children are school age or have grown up and the husband's salary is inadequate, and 70 percent would work when their children have grown up even if finances did not require it.

When we dichotomize the responses and trace the answers over the four years, the now-familiar patterns emerge. A noticeable segment develops motivation to work, a small number decide against working, and about one fifth of the class fluctuates, exhibiting inconsistent attitudes. Overall their desire to work grows somewhat, especially when there are no children or the children have already grown up. For example, the desire to work when children are grown and the husband's salary is inadequate shifts from 56 percent of freshmen to 70 percent of seniors. On the other hand, only about 7 percent of the class both as freshmen and as seniors say they would work with young children. So, after four years of thinking about it, the students do not change their ideas much where preschoolers are concerned.

In thinking about this issue, women cling to the idea that very young children require the mother's close attention, but they want some freedom. While the dominant view is that a woman must withdraw from the labor force at the birth of her first child, this does not mean that one must succumb to being a mere household drudge:

> I feel that a woman with a college background should keep up with changes in her field while she is raising her children. When her family has grown up she should play an active role in her community or re-enter her field so that there is no time in her life when she feels unfulfilled. I do believe a family comes before a career, however.

It is the minority of young women who plan to pursue their occupation continuously, who can place equal priorities on family and career:

> I feel that too many women are being wasted in the home. Most women are capable of combining the role of housewife/mother with a career. Most college-educated women need the stimulus of a part-time or full-time job in their chosen field to be of greatest value to themselves, their husbands and children.

Among this minority, there is still some ambivalence:

> If a woman has mental ability that would be useful in a profession, she should use it, not let it go to waste. A woman with any powers of organization should be able to manage family affairs and career. This is difficult though, because she should not undermine her husband's pride and his responsibility of supporting and caring for the family.

When students were presented with a hypothetical situation (involving no financial necessity for working) that forced them to choose one from among several alternatives including working, concentrating on home and family, or participating in clubs, hobbies and volunteer work, the limited pull of career is again apparent. In the first year of college, 38 percent choose to work full time or part time and in senior year 53 percent choose this alternative. But as Figure 3-4 reveals, a solid 25 percent prefer to concentrate on family- and leisure-oriented activities in all four years; only 14

Figure 4   Changes in Work and Home Preference

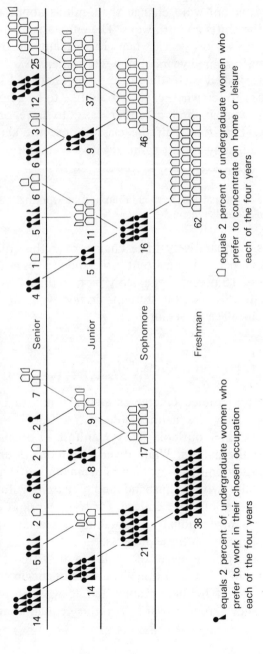

● equals 2 percent of undergraduate women who prefer to work in their chosen occupation each of the four years

◻ equals 2 percent of undergraduate women who prefer to concentrate on home or leisure each of the four years

percent consistently favor their chosen occupation. Among the 61 percent who change their minds about role preferences, the shifts go both ways. The emphasis on career comes largely in senior year, when 13 percent of the students convert after three years of non-work interests.

We also asked each student to project herself 15 years into the future to see whether she would like to be a housewife or a career woman, and in either case, to have or not have children. Less than half the class choose the career image, though this may reflect some negative connotations attached to the terminology. As one student put it:

> I want to be married, have children and be working, but "career woman" sounds hideous!

There is comparatively little change over the college years. Thirty-five percent consistently see themselves as housewives while only 16 percent repeatedly picture themselves as career women. In this case, the students do not even rally much to a career self-image by senior year.

The Game Plan for a Woman's Life

The women studied emerge as a special mix of the old and the new. They are neither solidly traditional nor patently pioneer in their outlook. They manifest an openness to the available alternatives. While diverse opinions flourish among seniors, the dominant preview of womanhood is an interesting, full life with a husband and children, with room for further education after college, for some work at convenient stages in a professional job, for hobbies, leisure, travel, and the chance to mesh these pursuits.

All these puzzle pieces of adult life are fitted together by adding them a few at a time. The students begin college with a desire to get further training and to work in professional fields. They grow toward a rather equalitarian view of marriage while they lose interest in delaying matrimony. They settle for professions that are women's fields, stressing personal care of preschool children so that work becomes a definite element of post-college life for the early and later stages of the family-life cycle. Family exigencies will dictate how much and at what stage a woman will fit work into her life. These, then, are mainly work-oriented but not career-centered people. They will enjoy interesting, stimulating jobs at times in life that permit or require working.

The college woman realistically expects to have varying responsibilities governed by her children's ages and by her husband's life style. Yet she cannot accurately predict what adulthood will bring. Hence she pursues a contingency orientation that looks like mere avoidance of commitment. But it is more than that. The contingency approach is also flexibility, which is built into women's socialization and planning. If we had studied only variables related to work, these special features of a woman's life would be overlooked. Looking solely at occupational choice or the high interest in graduate school, especially during senior year, makes it appear as if these women are very career-oriented, indeed. But by considering multiple facets of adult life, much change, oscillation, and indecision appear. Women's work and career interests must be viewed as integral parts of the congeries of life elements including family, leisure and education. In the next chapter, we present empirical evidence for such a more "total" view of womanhood.

4 Women Choose a Life Style, Not an Occupation

It would be a neat (but strange) world if all matters that hold for men were also true for women, and if women and men were totally alike. We say not only *viva la différence,* but also *considérons les différences*—let us take note of the differences. Behavioral scientists, predominantly male, have explained behavior through their own eyes and with their own theories. They assumed that women, like men, choose work to suit their abilities and interests. Especially the college educated supposedly seek the best fit between their personal qualities, interests and inclinations on the one hand and the requirements of the occupation on the other.

In the last chapter, we showed quite the opposite—that women's choices are not so concrete, not so specific, and far from wide-ranging. The extreme changeability of occupational choices, the lack of decisiveness in their plans, the resort to a short list of predominantly "women's" fields, the tendency to postpone a definite choice and to vacillate—all these tell us that while students perceive pressure to make decisions about their post-college lives, the particular occupation chosen is only one and perhaps not even the central component of their thinking about the future.

How important is occupation in a woman's adult life? The evidence nationally indicates the continued rarity of career women despite women's burgeoning participation in the labor force. The total numbers as well as the proportions of women in medicine, law, science, engineering and politics are small. Oppenheimer (1970) has shown that, until recently, the growth in women's gainful employment reflects primarily a large increase in the demand for women workers in particular fields, notably the white-collar jobs of teacher, secretary and clerk. The general expansion of the economy has augmented the employment of women in the service sector, in beauty shops, restaurants and the health fields. Many of these jobs can be entered easily, with little explicit advanced training required.

Women's personal circumstances and demographic factors have altered to produce more opportunity for work. Many more families now live in cities where jobs are available. In recent years, the lowering of fertility rates, the increase in age at first marriage, the introduction of better birth-control methods, and the longer life-span of women all combine to concentrate childbearing and child-rearing into the first half of women's lives. The increasing divorce rate, the continuance of widowhood status, and the low incomes many husbands receive propel some women, reluctantly, into work. One gains an impression, then, not of a surging increase in the career motivation of women, but of an upturn in the numbers who find they can or must work.

The character of women's socialization from childhood on helps to understand the rarity of their career commitment. Early in their development, women are taught to be flexible and open to the multiple adult roles they will play as wife, mother, hostess, club member, student or worker. These are roles that are defined largely by significant others, particularly one's spouse and children, rather than by the woman herself. The very pressure to remain open to life's options and to provide for family needs are the same forces that hinder women from active pursuit of careers. The socialization process reinforces this flexibility as desirable in order to prepare women mainly to serve others in the complex role constellations they assume and for which they receive little explicit preparation. This flexibility orientation fosters uncertainty and hesitation during college, so that when women should be ready to plan for adulthood, they cannot. They have learned to avoid commitments for so long that they readily avoid commitment to a career, and they also delay choosing an occupation. It is the onslaught of senior year, beyond which they can scarcely procrastinate, that pushes women to make such choices more specific. Most do plan to work at some time in their lives, but a miniscule few are prepared to plan for work as a central part of adult life equivalent to the centrality of family. The hesitancy to form career commitments, the emphasis on conventional women's fields, the frequent changes of heart and mind—we take these to reflect women's contingency orientation, a basic element in women's view of work.

For all these reasons, women's career aspirations must be viewed as integral to life style choices and commitments. Study of occupational choice alone obliterates the complexity of women's realistic attempts to anticipate and juggle their many roles. Thus occupational choice is merely a minor aspect of career aspirations for women. Instead, measurement of career aspirations should take into account both the role multiplicity that women anticipate and the changeability in their preferences.

In a concentrated review of the literature, we found no study in which career salience was measured as a central feature of life-style aspirations. Instead, there were numerous attempts to characterize the degree of women's specific desire to pursue a career. In a earlier decade, Empey (1958) thought that careers were a second choice for women, and that their planning was directed toward finding some occupation that would provide a career, if that became necessary. In the 1960s, evidence began to accumulate that women's aspirations are more varied. Shab (1967) concluded that college women were likely to view their adult role as a dual one including both marriage and a career. Studies focusing only on occupational choice tend to provide low estimates of the degree of career motivation of women; studies directed toward measuring career salience may over-estimate it.

Unfortunately, comparable methods of measuring degree of career orientation are infrequent. Measures of career salience typically stem from a single question, such as, "Do you want to be married, have a career, or both?" Occasionally women are divided into four or five categories; for example, those desiring marriage only, marriage with a deferred career, marriage and an immediate career, and career only (Watley and Kaplan, 1971). Sometimes career salience is defined broadly to include all women who express a desire to work after marriage. In other cases, only those who seek a masculine profession are counted. Our findings—the approach and withdrawal, the shrinking and expanding of work plans among women—suggest that single questions are not sufficient to encapsulate the wide range of career commitment among college women or the variety of factors that impinge upon their preferences. This led us to see if, by using several facets of adult life and viewing them through panel analysis, we could construct a measure that adequately taps women's complex aspirations.

Developing a Measure of Career Commitment

Since neither family nor work desires alone can predict which women will seek careers, we began with the assumption that career commitment must be tied to an intense desire to prepare for and to work in one's chosen occupation. The motivation to work must be strong enough for the woman to conceive of herself as a career woman and to arrange her life around work, at least to some degree. First we considered responses to two key questions, one asking these college women whether they would be willing to work at least part time even when their husbands earned enough so that money would not be a key work motive, and another asking them to project themselves into the future to see if they imagine themselves as career women 15 years after college. The answers to these two questions are highly correlated (Q = .86) so that those who define themselves as future career women also plan to work despite probable financial affluence. This correlation provides the first clear clue about the conceptual distinction between career-salient and homemaker-oriented women.

Second, the responses to these two questions given early in the fall semester of senior year were quite similar to later assessments of career salience taken during the spring semester. Despite this lapse of several months, the women are fairly consistent in their career orientation once they reach senior year.

Next we hypothesized that this distinction between career and non-career orientation should be reflected in a variety of other values and aspirations for adult life. Since career women are willing to make work a central part of life, their specific education, occupation and family aspirations should fit with and support their career concerns. These elements were included in the one measure of career aspirations in order to see if they are interrelated.

The Life Style Index

The composite measure of career aspirations that we developed is called the Life Style Index (LSI). We do not go into detail in this chapter, but present here only the rationale for the LSI and the results it yielded. Readers who are interested in the technical aspects of the Life Style Index—its development, reliability and validity—should turn to Appendix 2.

The LSI items reflect whether the woman wants to be employed under family conditions at various stages in the life cycle and without economic pressure to work, whether she values working in a self-directed occupation, and whether she plans to attend graduate school.

It is noteworthy that the occupational aspiration variables do not remain in the Life Style Index. The students' decisiveness about their occupational preference bears no relationship to career orientation; throughout college, the career salient feel no more and no less decided about their preferred occupation than the non-career salient. Preference for professional level work requiring an advanced degree is not associated with career salience in three of the four college years. Choice of a male-dominated field shows some relationship to career salience. In freshman, junior and senior years, the career-salient women tend to prefer occupations in which men predominate while the non-career women prefer traditional women's fields. These results are instructive in pointing up the limitations of occupational choice variables in explaining women's career orientation.

It is also important that generalized values concerning higher education—and especially values about type of work—play no strong part in women's life-style aspirations. Except for the preference to be free from close supervision, such values may be too general and remote from actual life choices, so that women's interest in a career is not strongly affected by them. This contradicts the evidence from the Cornell values study that career-oriented women resemble men in such work values (Rosenberg, 1957).

Given that the Life Style Index is internally consistent, how reliable is it as a measure of adult aspirations? Since the index was computed separately for each time period from freshman to senior years, the several indexes yield a kind of test-retest appraisal of their own reliability. The difficulty in assessing reliability that has plagued researchers is in the confounding of test with respondent. If a measure yields a high test-retest correlation, does this mean that the measure is consistently tapping the same dimension or that the respondents behave consistently? When the concern is with change, as in this study, one can rightly wonder whether high correlation coefficients signify that the test is reliable or that the respondents do not change much over time, or both. Using Heise's (1969) approach, this dilemma can be resolved by pulling apart the two aspects. This method utilizes retest scores from three different time points to separate the reliability of the test from the stability of responses.

When the Life Style Indexes for freshmen (T_1), sophomores (T_2) and juniors (T_3) are used, the reliability coefficient is .79. Using freshman, sophomore and senior Indexes, the reliability coefficient is .94, and the coefficient is .88 for the sophomore through senior Indexes. All of these are high.

By pairing each of the four time periods, six stability coefficients are estimated. The stability coefficients range from a low of .37 between freshman and senior years to a high of .89 between sophomore and junior years. The more time that elapses between tests, the more change that occurs. In other words, the least change in life-style aspirations occurs between any two contiguous years of college, while the most change characterizes the period between the first and last years.

The several reliability coefficients are generally higher than the stability coefficients. This indicates that the Life Style Index is indeed reliable, tapping the same configuration year after year. But the students lack consistency; they are rather changeable from year to year in their preferences.

Career Aspirations and Role Development

Having presented this description of the development of the Life Style Index, we can now highlight several issues. The measure's internal consistency and reliability for the sample studied suggest both its construct validity (Cronbach, 1960) and its utility in tapping college women's interest in pursuing careers. Assessment of the LSI's predictive validity must await a follow-up study of the actual life-style choices made by these women. The construct reflected in this measure is typically never considered unidimensional. Rather, most behavioral scientists and lay people alike assume that work, occupation, income, education, children, and husband each involves separate choices. Any attempt to combine these elements would acknowledge their multidimensionality. Now we argue that the LSI's internal consistency shows these choices to be highly and strongly interrelated. It also attests to the importance of taking such a more total view, the gestalt of a woman's adult life, both as college women foresee it and as adults actually enact their role constellations (Angrist, 1967).

Hints that career-salient women have special background, personality and cognitive features only tangentially related to occupation accrue from other sources also. Career-oriented women come from less conventional homes (Seward, 1945) or from families with conflicted relationships (Johnson, 1963; Rossi, 1967; White, 1959). In personality, the career oriented see themselves as more competitive, aggressive and managerial, contrasted with the more docile, self-effacing and cooperative image of the marriage-bound (Zissis, 1962). Specifically, high-need achievement and a strong desire for fame also characterize career-salient women (Masih, 1967). Finally, there is some evidence that career-oriented women are more able academically as measured by grades (Davis, 1966; Korn, 1967).

Such findings tell us the psychological characteristics associated with career orientation and non-career orientation; they say nothing about the connections between occupation and other aspects of a woman's life. Since these studies are done largely with cross-sectional samples, they reveal little about the *process* of women's role development during college, little about the extent of indecision and the variety of patterns that evolve during the college years. Later, we will detail some of the factors that differentiate career from non-career aspiring women, suggesting that career-oriented women do not simply reject conventional female aspirations. Rather, they are the products of family, educational and personal experiences that serve to enrich and broaden their outlook. Such girls are influenced to consider varied adult role combinations instead of exhibiting the typical primary striving for family status. The college years should contain such enriching influences, and, indeed, we already reported in the preceding chapter that college influences some women toward career as reflected in the increasing graduate school plans, the choice of an occupation, and the greater willingness to work after having a family.

Patterns of Change

The Life Style Index provides an even clearer picture of the general tendency for the whole class to become more career oriented over the four years. The great degree of change in aspirations is reflected in the rather low stability coefficient of .37 for the entire class. In addition, when we compare the mean LSI scores for freshmen with those of seniors, we find that the changes are not only great. It is also the case that the class as seniors is significantly more career oriented than as freshmen.* So the gross effect of passing through college is to foster career interests in these women.

Yet the great amount of variability, change and oscillation led us to wonder whether all of the 87 students were becoming more career oriented. And perhaps some students might lose rather than gain interest in career? Could any patterns of change be detected by considering all four years at the same time? Inspection of the Life Style Index scores suggested that, while the class as a whole seemed to score

---

*For the cohort of 87 students as freshmen, the mean LSI score and the standard deviation are 4.79 and 2.79, respectively; for seniors, the mean LSI score and standard deviation are 6.21 and 4.83 respectively. The t-ratio is 3.78; with 86 degrees of freedom, the difference is statistically significant at $p = .001$.

higher each year, some individuals were oscillating within a narrow range and others were declining. A closer look showed that the changeability could be reduced to five patterns to characterize subgroups within the class.

We shall see that the student patterns of change and consistency provide a basis for characterizing five types:

• the Careerists, or consistent career aspirers oriented to combining career with family roles in adult life

• the Non-careerists, or consistent non-career aspirers oriented primarily to family roles with some work and leisure pursuits

• the Converts to career aspirations who begin college without career orientation but move toward career interests by sophomore, junior or senior years

• the Defectors from career aspirations who are career oriented as freshmen and even thereafter but shift to non-career orientation by senior year

• the Shifters, inconsistent or changeable women whose life-style aspirations vary from year to year, lacking clearcut direction to or away from career orientation.

Types of Students

To arrive at the several types in terms of their representation in the class, we computed Life Style Index scores for each of the four years separately and then dichotomized at the class median for a given year. Scores at the median and above were considered high or career-oriented, scores below the median were low or non-career oriented. Patterns of the four-year sets of dichotomized scores for each girl were used to derive the five student types.

For the 87 students, the five types are distributed as follows:

Careerists	Non-careerists	Converts	Defectors	Shifters
18%	33%	22%	13%	14%

We then checked to see if the mean scores on the Life Style Index differed for each student type between freshman and senior years.* We found that only the Shifters, as might be expected, change randomly. They are a small segment of the class, 14 percent, who oscillate between career and noncareer orientation throughout college. Again, as might be predicted, the Defectors decrease in their LSI scores, so that by senior year their career aspirations have declined considerably.

The remaining three groups increase noticeably in LSI scores. The Careerists begin college with high aspirations, and these become even higher by the fourth year. The Converts begin college with low LSI scores but these grow significantly to high career aspirations in the last year. Ironically, the Non-careerists also increase significantly between the first year and the fourth year in their career aspirations. But their distinctive quality is that they remain low scorers in an absolute sense: they stay low on the LSI (below the median) and never score as high as the Converts or Careerists. Although the Non-careerists do develop some career orientation, they remain low aspirers relative to their classmates.

Clearly, the Non-careerists include the largest proportion

*The specific mean LSI scores with tests of significance for each student type for the first and last years are as follows:

	Careerists	Non-careerists	Converts	Defectors	Shifters
Freshmen:Mean	7.94	2.41	3.36	7.63	6.00
Senior:Mean	9.56	3.45	8.63	3.27	7.25
t-ratio*	3.22	2.53	14.45	6.31	1.43
	df=15	df=28	df=18	df=10	df=11
	p=.01	p=.02	p=.001	p=.001	p=N.S.

$$\text{*t-ratio} = \frac{\overline{X}_1 - \overline{X}_2}{\sigma_{\overline{X}_D}} \quad \text{where } \sigma_{\overline{X}_D} \text{ is the standard error of}$$

the mean difference. This is the t-statistic for matched observations (Senter, 1969, pp. 195-205).

of women in the class; that is, one third retain low aspirations in all four years. Another 13 percent "defect" or relinquish career interests by senior year. A rather small proportion of the class, 18 percent, maintain and increase their career orientation each year. Interestingly enough, the largest category comprises the "converts," the 22 percent who move radically to develop career aspirations during college. The Converts re-emphasize that there are strong forces for change that involve career planning. Although few women begin college as career aspirers, many arrive at such an orientation by the time they reach the last year.

The total proportion of strongly career aspiring seniors, including Careerists and Converts, adds to 40 percent of the class; this roughly equals the total who end up as largely non-career-oriented seniors, including Non-careerists and Defectors, or 46 percent. It is noteworthy, then, that neither type predominates in the senior class. Numerically, most substantial of all are the Careerists and Non-careerists, whose life-style aspirations change only within a limited range all four years; together, they comprise half the class. For these students, relatively little change is characteristic. They begin college and end it with approximately similar notions about their adult roles.*

Changeability During College

Colleges noticeably affect students—in personality, political outlook, attitudes and life styles (Feldman and Newcomb, 1969). But how great such impact may be has long raged as a leading dispute. In 1957, Jacob argued that colleges affect

---

*The variability among the five types is clear from analyses of variance both in freshman and senior years. The results show highly significant variation among the types at both time periods: for freshmen, the F ratio is 45.85, df = 4/82, p = .001; for seniors, the F ratio is 40.27, df = 4/82, p = .001.

their students little politically and intellectually. Later researchers contradicted this view with evidence that college alters not only attitudes and values but also personality (Newcomb et. al., 1967; Plant, 1962; Webster et. al., 1962). More recently, the burden of proof goes both ways: some students do change while others do not. Henry and Renaud (1972) report that some students may be "psychically foreclosed" with predetermined goals, never open to alternatives offered in the college experience. Others may approach college with a closed mind, but they become dramatically aware and open in the face of new situations. Still others pass through the "moratorium" of college, exploring and searching for self-growth within the college environment. And there are those consciously seeking to achieve their identity with flexibility, change and commitment.

Several important themes stand out from what we have reported so far. First, students *do* increase somewhat in the desire to work and even to pursue careers, but many women rest firm in their original family-centered aspirations. While we cannot compare this class of women to those at other universities nor with a control group of non-college women, it is clear that these women are high in the desire to work; the decision to work is virtually unanimous when there are no children or the children are at least school age and financial needs are compelling.

Second, by comparing these women to themselves each year, one can see that the class is far from homogeneous in role development. There are both converts to career and defectors from it. Still, the net changes on most of the specific variables reveal an increased career orientation.

A third conclusion is that the students are highly changeable during college, uncertain, ambivalent about their choices, trying to be pragmatic. This is especially evident from the percentage of students whose responses change from year to year without moving in any consistent direction. These fluctuations range from a low of about 15 percent who cannot make up their minds about graduate school to a high of 30 percent who vacillate between working and pursuing home-and-leisure interests.

Perhaps all this adds up to the conclusion that the study class reflects the cumulative effects of a college education. They feel and express the push toward the work world, picking a field and knowing "what you want to do," the pressures to get more education and for specialization after college. But they have to mesh these multiple interests in terms of the larger societal expectations for women. Thus, they adopt a contingency orientation: they are indecisive, vague, weighing out alternatives, stalling for time. In other words, direct commitments to advanced education and work are avoided as long as feasible, as is evident from the surge of graduate school and work plans in senior year. The avoidance of firm plans may simply reflect the desire for marital prospects to take shape *before* rather than *after* other plans (Turner, 1964). These women try to be flexible and open to fit the unknown spouse and with him an unknown life style (Douvan, 1960).

The great amount of indecision about adult life should not be attributed only to being female. High oscillation and shifting in adult role planning occur also among males in their occupational choice (cf. Holland, 1974). Now we must ask whether for women this shifting is bad or good, a sign of weakness or of strength, of drift or of openness to new possibilities. The shifting in aspirations is important because it suggests that higher education represents different things to different women.

The study class clearly incorporates a variety of types along the career-aspirations dimension. Some women remain relatively fixed in the desire to pursue work as a focal point of life—others rather invariably want domesticity. While both categories of women stay with their role outlook all four years, should we consider them similarly foreclosed or identically shut off from options? Or, in fact, any less constructive or less benefited by college?

We think not. When the subject is women's role development, we believe that even among the most unbending careerists and non-careerists much vacillation, worry and uncertainty prevail. These college women, despite their consistency, are inconsistent, groping for handles on the future they cannot predict, seeking sensible plans among hazardous contingencies. They exhibit the common ambivalence about a woman's life, whether to forge ahead or whether to hold back (Bardwick and Douvan, 1971). This struggle to complete the puzzle while the big pieces are missing haunts all the women.

That five types of women are distinguishable in even so small a class means that much more variation in aspirations prevails than one might expect. In the next chapter we portray the five types of women to highlight their distinctiveness. Each portrait is a composite of the women whose characteristics epitomize the type in family background, high-school experiences, behavior, attitudes, values and goals during college. We shall show that despite the differences among the five types, virtually all the women are undecided about many matters including college major, occupation, marriage and family, at least some of the time. Their fundamental changeability and ambivalence about life plans will open up the potential for influencing women to develop career interests—a possibility we will pursue later in the book. The portraits will expose the uncertainty about adult roles pervasive among college women regardless of career aspirations.

5 Five Variations and a Theme on Womanhood

The process by which girls learn to be women begins early in life. And it never ends. . . . When a girl comes to college, she rediscovers some of the old dilemmas: how to enjoy college but be practical, how to be feminine and still make her own choices, how to be independent from parents but still please them, how to cultivate her abilities but still avoid being aggressive, how to select a field of work but not seem competitive with men, how to plan her life but still remain open to men whose lives cross hers, how to . . . the thinking, weighing, hoping and judging go on and on. All college women are continuously juggling options; they anticipate that decisions and plans must follow soon on the heels of the college degree, yet some women may perceive the options differently.

How distinctive are the five types of women identified in the last chapter? Does the course of their role development proceed along separate channels? In sorting out the patterns from responses to the Life Style Index, we expected to find rather clearly defined mutually exclusive profiles. But as we analyzed questionnaires and interviews to portray total persons, we found the interweaving of variations on a theme, more like a symphony with movements than sharply etched portraits. So we must present what we found. Our purpose is to accent some important differences in the development process that unfolds during college. We dare not say that college causes these several patterns. We do suggest that the process involves alternative strategies, priorities and outcomes for Careerists, Non-careerists, Converts, Defectors and Shifters. Yet underlying the diversity is the common wrestling with being female, trying to act and choose what fits a woman, hoping to satisfy oneself and significant others.

The Careerist: Carol

Carol was a good student during high school; she not only made A's but felt that her teachers considered her outstanding. Her college grades are only fair at first—she begins with C's in freshman year, but obtains a B average after that. She believes that professors in her freshman courses look on her as only average, but in her last two years she thinks they view her as outstanding. She feels free to talk to them about course projects and assignments. Looking back at her freshman year, Carol describes "having several excellent professors" as the source of her greatest satisfaction.

As a freshman she expresses some well-formulated ideas about herself and about her goals in life. She recalls that her parents, who are Jewish, encouraged her occupational ambitions:

> I think both my parents have done a lot to motivate me. They are not telling me what to be interested in, but once I pick an interest, they are there to help me or push me or do about anything I need.

Her mother completed high school and attended a secretarial school for two years. She worked at secretarial and clerical jobs almost continuously during Carol's lifetime. Her mother was also moderately active in clubs and spent time on her hobbies. Carol's mother impresses her daughter as endowed with accomplishments and energy, but some talents remain untapped:

> My mother has a fantastic influence on me. When she got out of high school, she had to support her family. Yet every year she's taking a new course or reading piles of books or sculpting. This is very nice but if that intellect could have been directed, she'd be more satisfied as a person and be of greater use to society.

From the very beginning of college Carol is mainly concerned with pleasing herself in choosing a field of work. She wants to make up her own mind, but she is aware of several people who may have influenced her, among them a high-school English teacher and a social worker at the summer camp where she worked. To suit parental ideas of success and to seek financial reward are completely unimportant; she wants to find an occupation that allows her freedom and independence. Choosing a field that provides a secure future is grossly unimportant. In general, Carol tends not to depend on other people as sources of satisfaction, nor does she usually seek people out on her own initiative. She is more concerned with satisfying her curiosity and expressing her interests. This characterizes her conception of college education as well as her notions about work.

Graduate study in English is among the plans Carol enunciates as a novice in college. She has no paid work experience until the summer before college and feels undecided about exactly what occupation to pursue or what major to pick. She considers writing since she did well in English during high school. Her choice of occupation is very like the kinds of fields her friends are choosing. Both her boyfriends and her girl friends prefer fields nearly all of which would require graduate or professional school preparation—research in chemistry, medicine, teaching, law, biology, design, psychology. Further, these are fields in which men predominate. Thus Carol and her coed friends are unconventional in this respect—they prefer occupations atypical for women.

With her occupational interests still tentative, Carol approaches college holding great expectations. She looks to the higher educational experience as a way to expose new possibilities and to challenge her. But freshman year is disappointing:

> The school let me down in a lot of respects. Socially and academically. A lot of stuff seemed basic and trivial.

Junior year begins to provide the satisfaction she seeks:

> I'm getting more involved in my major. I've started to think about graduate school. English is a field in which you need a master's degree, and maybe a doctorate. The field is so wide.

The job she holds in the English department amplifies her involvement in the field. It is more than the subject matter that intrigues her now, it is the people around whom she works:

> I like the professor I work for. I'm meeting a lot of people in the department and seeing it in action. Some of the instructors are really exciting people, doing important things. Professors get to know you, and to know your work. I learn a lot from them and get to be friends with them. I've even found some who can give me a good recommendation.

Her senior year is the most challenging of all:

> This has been the best year. My interests are very much involved in my department. My grades were excellent and my courses very good, not as superficial as earlier ones. Papers were required rather than final exams. This is a good indication of depth in a course.

Still a remnant of dissatisfaction remains with her courses and classmates:

> I'd like my classes to be more challenging, to be above me. I

would work harder and be more motivated. I find that students compete for grades and trivial things that don't matter to me.

One element of her academic dissatisfaction is the desire for more exposure to what she calls "the male viewpoint":

When I was in high school, I thought of an all-girl school as an advantage. Really, I think it is disadvantage. You need a male viewpoint not for any social reason, but it's an intellectual male viewpoint that's lacking in a lot of classes.

Although she is little involved in campus activities and particularly shuns the round of sorority-fraternity life, she makes feeble attempts to take part in extracurricular activities:

I didn't join any groups in freshman year. I didn't date because of my grades. In sophomore year I was vacillating. I was more interested in finding myself and my field of work. I don't belong to clubs now. In a way I regret this, I keep saying I will belong but it's something I have to force an interest in. I would rather concentrate on my studies.

At first she dates around:

It's difficult to meet boys on this campus. I usually accept blind dates. They're okay if you really want to get out.

But for a while in junior year she goes with one boy:

Usually we do something on Saturday night. But on Friday night I try to work. We see each other whenever we can, like he comes over to talk for an hour. Or we take an hour off and go to the museum. We don't goof around very much.

In the last semester of senior year she perceives the changes in herself during college as follows:

I was more aware of campus life as a freshman. I was much more concerned about making friends and getting a date. I was probably scared and insecure. But now things tie in; my friends are in my department. They are not separate from everything. The courses I take seem to complement one another. I've learned a lot in four years.

Senior year brings an even stronger career outlook for her future. She always felt sure she wanted to marry and as a freshman hoped to do so upon graduation. She had at that point also projected that she would want to have three children. All through college she imagines herself working at least part time, even after marriage and the birth of her children. But as a senior she feels definite about planning to work full time while her children are still young. At that stage she thinks a qualified nurse or housekeeper could provide suitable child care. Married life entails sharing of tasks and responsibility in her view. While earlier she was undecided about this, as a senior she fully expects her husband to participate with her in the household tasks such as cooking and cleaning, as well as in raising children. At the end of the senior year she is not certain whom or when she will marry, but her opinions on this matter are clearcut:

I wouldn't ever consider stopping work to have children. I think that is a crime in our society to slave all these years and become a productive writer and then say I'll see you in 15 years after my children grow up. If I want children, they're just going to have to be worked in. I can't say for sure because I've no desire to have children right now. The thought of being a housewife makes me say "never" because woman's intellect should be used to capacity. It shouldn't be used in the kitchen.

Her occupational aim has crystallized:

I feel older now and more knowledgeable. I went into English in freshman year because it seemed a good idea. Now it is more than that, it is something I want to make a career of. I don't think anyone has really guided me. It's a subtle thing: the whole department influenced me, especially Dr. S., whom I work for, and my specific instructors. I hope some day to go into a college faculty, to write and teach.

If I go into this field I expect fully to find people who are as enthusiastically interested and hard-working as the ones I've seen in the department and in my summer jobs.

The Non-Careerist: Nancy

One dominant feature of Nancy's personality is that she counts on others to push and channel her activities and interests. She sees the world as fairly well defined by people around her with few matters open to question or doubt. She was well adjusted in her all-girl Catholic high school. Her only problem at that stage was to maintain both the grades and the motivation to go to college as her parents expected:

My parents wanted me to go to college. If not, I'd have taken a year in secretarial school.

Not only did her parents direct her into college, they also specified which one, because: "my father went to this school and he wanted me to go here." Further, they disapprove of her initial choice of biology as a major. So after freshman year, she switches to home economics. Looking back on that, Nancy reflects:

Family, friends, relatives, people who had known me for a long time always expected me to go into home economics—even when I was in high school.

The decision to concentrate on the fashion design and retailing option is more explicitly her own:

I sort of picked it by eliminating other things. And I've always liked work with clothes.

At the end of sophomore year, Nancy feels certain she will
not change majors:

> There's really nothing else I'm interested in. I cannot think of
> another major I would be interested in learning or capable of
> succeeding in.

In Nancy's family, boys are expected to pursue careers.
Her mother had never worked after marriage. She explains
the family's conception of what is appropriate for a woman:

> I have been taught that a woman should concentrate on her
> family and her home. What a woman does in the family should
> come first ahead of everything else.

During high school, Nancy held this image of a woman's life
and she continues to see it similarly all during college. She
has no contact with the work world until the last two years
of college when she works as a sales clerk in a department
store. This comes as part of her teachers' encouragement that
students in the retailing major get such experience.

Two matters take up most of Nancy's time in college:
sorority and schoolwork. With these two things she says: "I
have enough to occupy my time." The sorority gives her a
great deal of satisfaction:

> I feel very close to the girls in the sorority. They're the most
> wonderful girls I ever met. I enjoy being with them.

She believes that the sorority makes dating and meeting boys
a lot easier. But she begins to date one boy quite steadily in
sophomore year:

> Through him I've met lots of guys. Other girls complain that it's
> hard for them to meet people. Our home economics classes have
> all girls. I guess it's because I've been dating one person that I
> don't notice it.

Schoolwork is sometimes pleasing, sometimes disappointing to her. Her main problem academically is that she finds it hard "to concentrate and study for long stretches of time." But she is generally satisfied with her major.

> There's nothing else I was interested in, maybe that's why I chose it. I've had liberal arts courses and electives. I've had specifics to prepare me for an occupation.

Still she ponders what she will do after college. As a sophomore, Nancy explains that this preoccupation is common among her girl friends:

> We talk about whether we are getting enough out of school. Is this worthwhile? Wouldn't it be horrible if we all got married the day we graduated and never used these four years? Would our education be a waste of time? My one problem is that I'm doubtful about what I want to do and what I can do. I need two more years to think about it.

As they consider the kinds of fields they might pursue, Nancy and her female friends always prefer women's occupations. At the beginning of college her acquaintances are considering secretarial work, teaching or home economics. As time wears on, her close friends are all in home economics and specializing in one of its subfields—nutrition, textiles, retailing or teaching. By contrast, her male friends are choosing academic fields such as economics, mathematics and computer sciences, or professions such as law or engineering. Nancy's preference for a woman's field reflects her values about work. She cares little about making a lot of money. Nor is she concerned with work that would allow her to use her special abilities. She feels uncertain about what her abilities actually are. It is important that when she is ready to work, the job will provide a secure future.

With the advent of senior year, she comments extensively

on her major, trying to evaluate its benefits and shortcomings:

> I would like to work for a department store as a buyer. Maybe after I get into it I won't like it, but I'm interested in that.

Her plans to work as a buyer are still very tentative. Her sorority activity diminishes since she becomes engaged and expects to marry right after graduation—she had always hoped to marry early and feels ready for it. Marriage is a "drawback" to her work interests:

> I'm going to get married and I will have to work, but I'm not sure what kind of job I want to take. I've chosen to get married and I know I can't have a career and raise a family. I don't think I can be successful with both. There are jobs and there are careers. In one you build your life around the career. In the other you build the job around your life. I'd better take the job and make married life the career.

The Convert: Connie

Connie was a top student in high school and considered outstanding by her teachers. Academic work in college was another matter:

> I got the jolt of my life when I found out about the work. But now I'm adjusted to it and I keep at it.

By sophomore year she gets B grades and begins to feel she is a bright student in the eyes of her college professors. She discovers to her great satisfaction that she can "get good grades without being a bookworm":

> I enjoyed classwork and got satisfaction from doing well in a class which I knew was difficult.

Each year her grades go up and she grows more aware of her

academic ability. These good grades and talks with the faculty reinforce her self-concept as a capable student.

From the start of college, home economics is her major. However, Connie is vague about occupational interests. She considers public relations, psychological measurement, teaching or library work. The latter seems to combine her desire to pick a field of work with her urge to help others. The trouble with home economics as a major in Connie's view is that it fails to point her toward any concrete occupation:

> There's nothing you can do with it besides teaching. Unless, of course I get further degrees. . . .

So it is that in sophomore year Connie begins to feel ambivalent about her choice of major. But she does not switch fields. Instead she begins contemplating graduate or professional school. For a while she prefers to become a nutritional chemist. However, eventually she returns to her earlier notions of dietetics. Again, her choice lacks conviction. For one thing, she wants to be married by about twenty-one or twenty-two years of age. And she worries about how to fit family life and work together. As a freshman, Connie wants to incorporate a little of everything in her adult life: working part time in a chosen occupation, belonging to some clubs, doing volunteer work and being a housewife with several children. The following year she thinks more about career. It now seems clear that she can see herself in 15 years as a career woman, married and with children. But she stipulates that she would not do anything "at the risk of depriving my children of the attention and love they need."

With the advent of the senior year, several experiences combine to move her toward career planning:

> When I started college, I did not really conceive of going to graduate school. I thought I would probably become a nutritionist and I figured if I got married, I would take 10 or 15 years to raise a family and then go back to work. Right now I don't see that.

With the training I have now and after a few years more of school, there is no reason why I shouldn't work. For a long time I was hesitant because of all the nasty things you read in magazines about the effects on children. I don't think there would be any detriment to the children, so I don't see why I should impair myself.

In reflecting on her own ideas about women's roles, she describes her mother's situation now that the three children are out of the house:

My mother has devoted 25 years of her life to us. She does not have anything else to do. I think a person stops growing that way. I would not want this to happen to me.

At the close of her college years, Connie knows she will go to graduate school "to get a master's degree for sure." Her hopes for a career are clear but her actual plans still lack complete definition:

I intend to work after graduate school, to make a full-time career. Obviously it's a little complicated. Things are pretty well up in the air. I intend to work when I get out. Whenever I marry, I intend to have children but I won't stay home with them for 5 or 10 years. If I go through college and get an advanced degree, at that point it's silly not to use it. From people I know and from what I've read, it is quite possible that I would be able to work and have children. There shouldn't be any real conflict with it as long as my husband was cooperative in the matter.

The Defector: Debra

Debra is from a well-to-do Protestant family living in the same metropolitan area as the university. She wants the experience of being away at college so she stays in the dorm during all four years. But she enjoys going home frequently, usually leaving campus Sunday morning and returning to school on Monday. She looks up to her parents. Her father is a successful physician—Debra says she hopes to marry an M.D. some day. Her brothers are younger and still at home. She speculates that perhaps they will follow their father's footsteps. Her mother is devoted to homemaking and to encouraging the various pursuits of family members.

College is a very significant place for Debra. She values highly the contacts with varied types of people comprising the rubric of campus life. But she centers her activities in her sorority. This satisfies her dating needs and provides many close friends.

Debra had been a good student in high school and she is determined to do well in college. Although she works industriously as a freshman, her grades are mainly C's and she finds herself just an average student compared with class-mates. As a sophomore Debra decides:

> I was working hard and not getting results even when I knew the material. Now I realize it is not so all-important to get grades. There are other things.

But this decision fails to dampen her will to achieve as best she can. To graduate from college is a crucial goal. Her parents expect it and she herself never wavers in that aim. Since less studying does not threaten that goal, she relaxes about being an average student.

Along with the relaxation in her academic outlook, Debra's major field and work interests shift after the freshman year. Her first plan is a major in nutrition as the basis for a career in dietetics. As a sophomore she moves into the home economics major, staying with it for the remainder of college. Still, she retains a strong interest in the foods and nutrition area; she takes as many such courses as fit her schedule. The switch in majors is directly related to her new view of occupational possibilities. For one thing, dietetics calls for a year of internship *after* the bachelor's degree while teaching certification would come *with* the degree. And Debra wants to be practical:

It seems silly to go to college for four years and not be able to do something when you graduate. I want to learn something so I can make money and support myself.

But money is not a key motive for choosing education. After freshman year, she attaches little importance to work that provides high income. Nor does she care about expressing her talents through work. By junior year, Debra reasons:

Teaching will give me the kind of work and hours I would like. I think it is a good job for a woman, with more security in case I need to go back to work when I'm older. It would be easier to get into education than into dietetics and I don't think the work is as physically hard as being a dietitian.

Since she had no work experience before college and knew little about dietetics, Debra takes a summer job after freshman year in a hospital kitchen. The long hours, hard work and hot steam tables clinch her decision to forget that occupation.

Further changes in her thinking accompany Debra's altered work interests. When college began she thought of herself as an eventual career woman. She could picture herself 15 years later as employed part time in her chosen field even though she would be married and have children. She expected to defer marrying until she had a foothold in her career. In sophomore year, these ideas are abandoned. Her aspirations the last three college years are consistently domestic. She hopes to marry upon graduation, to become a housewife with several children, focusing her energies on home and family, perhaps with some time for hobbies. She always strongly believed that a mother should personally care for her young children, and she continues to hold that belief.

With the advent of senior year she has no marriage plans and it is clear to Debra that she will have to work. She notes that most of the girls in her major plan to take jobs right after graduation. She rationalizes:

I would like to work for a few years. If I did not, it would be like throwing four years down the drain.

In the spring, Debra begins to worry about her job prospects:

What am I going to do come June? I don't know what to do. If I don't get a job I may go back to school.

Part of the worry is whether she will marry and part involves what kind of work to seek. She hesitates to become a teacher for fear she will lack social and dating contacts:

Education is an insurance policy for later on. It would give me something to fall back on. But I don't want to teach right now. I want to get out in the business world and meet people. Ideally, I would like a traveling job, but one with a home base.

Thus, although she feels decided about teaching as her occupational preference, it gets relegated to later life lest she lose out on opportunities to meet a mate. Reconsidering dietetics, Debra finds it also unsuitable:

I don't think it is a field you can re-enter easily. They want people who can work full time and long hours to make a career in institutional dietetics, perhaps to become a supervisor. They won't rehire someone at age 40 and make her a supervisor. With teaching there is no such gap. You can always substitute teach.

Now she muses over several other possibilities, such as becoming a home demonstrator with an appliance company, or working as a lab technician in a foods industry, or retailing or consumer education. Although she had been subject to their expectations more emphatically at the start of college, Debra feels it pertinent to consider her parents' ideas about her post-college job choice. Especially where location is concerned, Debra hesitates to leave home to go to another city:

At first I thought my parents want me to take a job in the same

city because I have always been close to them. Now they realize
that I am going to leave if I want to. But I don't know if I will or
not.

Thus she approaches graduation with overriding uncertainty
and confusion—what to work at and where and to what
purpose remain pressing problems. With marriage as her only
definitive goal and no husband in sight, she is at loose ends
about everything else, fearing her own insecurity and
dreading any work that may require too much commitment
or reduce her marriage chances.

The Shifter: Sandy

Sandy was a very competent student in high school. She does
not find course work or studying difficult when she gets to
college. From freshman year forward she finds learning an
enjoyable experience. At first "learning fascinating things
from professors and courses" constitutes her greatest satisfaction. As she moves through college, Sandy wants to savor
people as well as learning. She exerts more effort to make
new friends and finds this rewarding.

Initially, Sandy thinks college is "a big nebulous thing that
goes on and on." Her parents had not been to college and she
had few preconceived ideas of what to expect. She thinks it
important to be a good student and values being considered
so by her teachers. But beyond the serious intention of
obtaining the bachelor's degree, Sandy is unsure what she
expects from college. Neither has she any certain goals for
after college.

While schoolwork is rarely a problem, Sandy experiences
difficulty during the first two years in her social milieu. For a
while she is "just gathering impressions." Then she works to
become part of college life:

I tried hard to integrate myself into the dorm and the school. I

joined several groups and made a few good friends. I was just
learning what I really wanted and where I could find a place in the
school. I used to be more contented studying, but eventually I
resolved my difficulty. I dropped out of most activities so they
would not be an obligation. Just having my friends left me free.
The school now seems such a friendly place. There's a diversity of
people. You just accept people for what they are.

With English as her declared major in freshman year,
Sandy imagines she will become a writer or a journalist. The
choice is a difficult one to make; nor is it a choice completely
her own. Sandy's father is the one person who most helped
her decide on this during high school. However, now friends
and teachers begin to play a part, too. Besides these sources
of influence, Sandy feels encouraged by her performance:
"English is the only thing I do exceptionally well in."

Still, there remains a vagueness and wavering about this
major until sophomore year when she switches to social
science. By this time Sandy registers what her friends and
dates are interested in. She now looks to them as well as to
her parents for help in choosing an occupation.

Her decision to change majors is influenced by a summer
job. Most summers Sandy had vacationed with her family.
She had no work experience until freshman year when she
and several friends worked with children in the poverty
program alongside teachers and social workers:

It was interesting and so rewarding. I was seeing people doing
things. This made me eager to do something just working with
people.

At this point, Sandy shifts her preference to social work and
gives up the idea of journalism. Her decision includes some
doubt about going on to graduate school.

As she contemplates a field of work, Sandy hesitates. Even
as a sophomore, she wonders if she could make a career of
social work or any other related field. For a while, she plans
to work right after college and delay graduate school. And

she imagines that after marrying and having children she will work part time in social work or counseling, assuming that she would somehow go to graduate school before having a family. In her discussion about the social science major, Sandy explains:

> I enjoy my major. I like writing papers and reading. I'm getting an education. I want an education and I'm content with what I'm getting. But I'm not going to make a career of it.

By senior year, Sandy is more uncertain than ever about the after-college life:

> It is hard for me to decide what to do with my life. It is terribly problematic. It is the end of the four years in which there was so much security. Now I don't know what I'm doing.

Work, graduate school, marriage are all possibilities, but none definite:

> I would like to finish graduate school. Whether I will ever work or not, I don't know. I imagine I'll be married in the next year or two. If the situation warranted my working, then I definitely would. If I were bored with housework, I would probably work. I would not work if I had enough to do. I'm not a typical career person. I'm not that dedicated.

With no specific plans for after graduation, Sandy still centers on family as a goal. This is the pivotal projection for her adult life:

> When you take the responsibility of a family it is your duty to do it as well as you can and devote as much time to it as possible.

While she remains interested in work at some stages of her life she maintains that:

> . . . home and family are probably the most important things a woman ever has to do. Most men are not willing to do the dishes and run the sweeper. A man just cannot do these things. I don't

know what to do about children. A career really interferes with children and children interfere with a career. I would not want my children to be taken care of by anyone else and feel they are unloved by me.

If Sandy's ideas about family life change little during college, nearly everything else does, especially her notions about people and about herself. She is articulate and talkative in describing the changes in herself as "enormous" and her general philosophy of people as "completely changed":

College made me realize that I didn't have any closed answers. Everything is a matter worth investigating and looking into further. There are no pat answers. The people I met in college have a fluid outlook on things. I used to believe in free will. Now I've changed my moral and political opinions. My attitudes to myself, my friends, my parents are different. I understand now that there are a lot of things people can't control and that makes me more tolerant.

For Sandy, then, the college years are intellectually stimulating and personally enlightening. They yield personal enrichment and a broader outlook. But they add little to clarifying future goals or to altering the paramount place of family.

What Do the Portraits Show?

One striking impression gained from the student portraits is the extent to which no type is an absolute. The labels were derived from life-style aspiration scores and focus only on changeability or lack of change in career orientation. The portraits demonstrate this matter well. Within each type there is some variability: the changers are fixed in some aspects of career orientation, the non-changers are changeable in some aspects. Nevertheless, each type has its predominant change pattern with a loose constellation of associated characteristics.

The Careerist is the sole chooser of a male-dominated

occupation. She picks a field much like that of her boyfriends. She is strongly affected by her mother's example as a well-educated, active woman who hòlds a job and participates in community groups. She shuns sorority during college. Her motivation is to find work that is personally satisfying and at a high level; her field choice need not suit her parents' success notions, provide security or high salary or center on helping others. She views child-care as something in which other competent adults can assist or replace her temporarily. To the careerist, college is the place and time for choosing and shaping her life's work.

The Non-careerist is clear in her goals: she is totally family oriented and concerned with selecting a mate. She gets attached to a male by senior year. She has little enthusiasm about schoolwork and is rather unstimulated by it. She is tied to the university primarily through the friends and social activities centering in the sorority. Her view is of work as a practical means to achieve security when and if she will ever need to work. Family is her career.

The Convert develops the desire for a career mainly because she discovers her academic skills and feels rewarded by her professors' view of her as a bright student. She prefers marrying early rather than waiting. By working in a "woman's" profession with convenient hours she feels any potential career-home conflict is avoided.

The Defector is set on working at not too high a level in a field considered appropriate for women, and one which will fit her parents' ideas of success. These reasons are reflected in her choice of teaching. Higher education is very important for achieving the college degree itself and as preparation for a job, but she views any postgraduate training as a last resort. She defines her work aims mainly by default. Marriage is her key aspiration. Job holding is both a means to that end and a way to help pass the time until marriage.

The Shifter is traditional in her ideas of husband-wife domestic responsibilities and seems confused about her goals. She looks to higher education for enjoyment, stimulation and a way of clarifying things. She remains conventional in her sex-role conceptions, but college provides the arena in which she develops a broader philosophy about people and life in general.

While the five portraits show differences in important respects, they also overlap in some ways. They describe students in a private, fairly selective school with a limited number of majors offered, who are largely middle class and competent students. Differences in academic performance and social characteristics, while present, are not dramatic. Furthermore, in two aspects of adult women's roles, the entire study class clusters within a narrow spectrum: They all desire to marry and have children, and most expect to work at some time in their lives. They all reflect a constant struggling with hopes, plans and the reality of life as a woman. They all stress the centrality of family life, yet they wrestle with its indeterminacy involving factors beyond their control. Such are the elements which the women studied share.

Within this homogeneity, there is important diversity in priorities, inclinations and influences on adult-role aspirations. While the college years move many in the class to convert career plans, that outcome is by no means overwhelming. Some women move away from career concerns and others oscillate, remaining unsure of their goals. Most striking is the finding that there are many students whose career orientation or lack of it remains quite constant all through college.

Only the consistent Careerist seeks to plan her adult life around family and work; the Convert comes to that plan by the end of college. On a continuum of career orientation, the five types would range from the Careerist at one end to the Non-careerist at the other, with the Convert, Shifter and Defector between the two extremes. Whether time will prove this true is, of course, another matter to be ascertained in a follow-up study. Given a few years in the world, each type of woman may change from the pattern she established during college. If their college portraits persist into adult life, the Careerists and Converts should become professional career women, the Non-careerists and Defector housewives, the Shifters, seekers who try a bit of everything.

So far we have stressed the homogeneity these women exhibit and their diversity, common dilemmas and distinctive aspirations. In the chapters that follow we will look more carefully at the diversity. First we survey proposed explanations of women's choices and find them somewhat lacking, especially those that purport to explain occupational choice. Then we highlight the focal distinctions between the career oriented and the non-career oriented, inspecting their backgrounds, attitudes and experiences in order to unravel the factors that foster career aspirations and those that discourage them.

6 False Explanations of Women's Career Choices

The mythology about women and careers starts this way. Women appear over-all less committed to work than men. Men expect to spend most of their adult life in paid employment. Since their life style, status and their feelings of well-being depend specifically on the particular occupation they pursue, men are expected to give careful thought to the business of choosing an occupation. Since women's energies are more probably consumed by household (unpaid) work and motherhood, and the portion of their lives devoted to work is less than men, they can afford to approach their occupational choice more frivolously. Lotte Bailyn puts the problem a little more succinctly:

> That a man will spend at least one third of his adult life in gainful work is a premise on which the plans for his life are based. But for a woman, society creates not a decision but the necessity for a choice. She must decide whether to include work in her plans and if so how much of her life she should devote to it. If the answer is that she will include work in a serious way, she then arrives at the point at which the career thinking of men begins (Bailyn, 1964, p. 702).

The first half of this book portrayed how winding and uncertain, how varied and hesitant the choice process is for college women. Work is not the sole issue—the students want to work for some time in their lives and the college experience encourages them to do so. So women try to select an occupation. It is in the choice process that women express their broader concern for adult life, a concern which men hardly face: how to mesh marriage, parenthood, personal interests and career aspirations.

In trying to make sense of women's life style choices, social scientists accept the conventional wisdom that, after all, women do not want careers. Or they take the argument another step to: women cannot succeed in careers. With these two fell swoops women's interests, abilities and potential are simply wiped out.

The history of this conventional wisdom is ancient but it lacks nobility. It stems from dogma and traditions more than from objective analysis of "what is." After World War II there was a widespread feeling that the sexes in America were at last becoming equal. That war opened the military's door to substantial numbers of female Americans but still in segregated arrangements—as munitions workers (remember Rosie the Riveter?), as nurses, typists and office workers. Women would always be excluded from combat, they would continually fill so-called women's occupations and they would live mainly in sex-segregated groups. In 1972, the U.S. Air Force had the highest concentration of women personnel among all the military branches—still they remain in traditional roles (Goldman, 1973).

Perhaps because of women's sizeable role in that war effort, behavioral scientists began to notice that family life might change if women worked on a large scale, that women might need alternative roles both within the family and outside it. The trumpeting of family life, the beauty of the small intimate nuclear family, and the centrality of women to domesticity filled the 1950's like a catechism. The idea that women found full expression within the home was accompanied by recognition that housewifing and mothering leave room for some variation. In the classic statement of the time,

Talcott Parsons (1954) enlarged the woman's world to include the "glamor" role and the companionate role—of course, these focused on how she complimented her husband, the star of the show. Nevertheless, this helped crack the solid hausfrau image and made possible the discovery that women can have diverse interests and role preferences.

Why had behavioral scientists ignored women's endeavors outside the home? Had they read about the suffragettes at the Seneca Falls Convention in 1920? Had they heard about Jane Addams' establishment of settlement houses and the founding of insane asylums by Dorothea Dix in the fast growing urban centers at the turn of the century? Did they know about women working to support their unemployed men in the Great Depression Years?

Even when they would not or need not work, educated women always sought something interesting to do. More than that, in every time and place of American history, the educated cultivated classes of women forged alternatives for themselves through creative work in their homes or communities. But, constrained by conventional expectations, they had to remain unobtrusive, to keep their place, to hold to acceptable roles. To do something useful, to help others and to express one's self—these were the logical amalgam of their education and their female weltanschauung.

A chronical of the first seventy years of Vassar's existence reveals this blend of striving among such elite women. Contemporary letters and manuscripts in 1869 and 1870 tell of the early rejection of "poky lectures" and the constant search "to feel capable." The students write of rushing off to the library to read on current events and political economy, and of concern with learning, knowing, doing (Plub and Dowell, 1961; Scott, 1971).

Of course, these were the aristocratic daughters of their time. Yet their model of stretching and pushing against sex role constraints prevails to this day. Economists have found no way to measure or value the gourmet cooking, the artistic decorating, the elegant hostessing, the fine sewing today's women pursue at home. Nor are there sociological scales to weigh the contribution to community and society. Women rarely expect payment for their efforts—they consider home-making and volunteer work a duty and often a pleasure. Women may treat philanthropic work like a career-devoting time, energy and talent and obtaining considerable satisfaction from such work (Ross, 1958). As in other spheres, women's efforts in voluntary organizations receive little public recognition and their special participation patterns remain scantly studied (Smith and Freedman, 1972).

Women's expectations for themselves seem to incorporate both society's demands and women's own drive to excel even within the traditional spheres. A study of women's instrumental role performance after psychiatric hospitalization (Angrist et. al., 1968) reports the surprising finding that the former patients have high expectations for their own performance in the domestic and leisure realms; in fact, their self-expectations are much higher than their husbands actually expect. When the former patients are compared with their normal neighbors (who had never received any psychiatric treatment), the same pattern holds: these "normal" wives also expect more of themselves than do their husbands.

A careful analysis of how mothers spend their time reveals the same concern to stretch themselves as well as to benefit their children. No matter what the family income permits for hiring household help, mothers invest a substantial amount of time in child care (Leibowitz, 1972). And for college educated mothers the time allocated for child care is even greater than it is for the less educated. Astonishing as they may seem, both employed and unemployed mothers spend about the same amount of time on child care when their children are very young (Walker, 1973).

In studies of college alumnae who were full-time home-makers, Searls (1966) found that the women who enjoy homemaking and who feel they have mastered the skills required for household and childcare tasks, are more active in leisure pursuits both inside and outside the home. So their

leisure activities are not an escape from domestic incompe-
tence or dislike of homemaking—they can and want to do
more than just homemaking. Indeed, they exploit various
opportunities to pursue personal interests: Women who can
afford it, hire household help to free themselves for several
hours a day; housewives with young children and without
paid help carve out in-home activities, such as music or art or
writing; women with school-age children spend more time on
community based activities, including civic, religious and
educational groups (Angrist, 1967).

Although all these studies underline women's special
role-juggling and accommodation to marriage and motherhood, theories of occupational choice evolved as if these
matters did not exist. The male world of work is the context,
the achievement-success orientation and the open society are
the assumptions. On these, the models of career choices build
and try to fit women. But alas, we shall show that the
theories are woefully inadequate, totally inappropriate for
women.

Studies of career planning among college students most
often center on one matter: the particular occupation
chosen. Consequently a large body of theoretical and
empirical literature has developed which purports to explain
occupational choice. The central proposition is that occupational choice involves a process whereby the child thoroughly
explores the numerous possibilities, gives full consideration
to all of his or her inclinations and interests, and attempts to
match personal characteristics with an occupation. Exploration and consideration of options make the process exciting,
with the maturing adult narrowing the alternatives to
eventually select one occupation for which he or she is best
suited. Much of this viewpoint derives from the study of men
and while it seems largely inapplicable to women, we would
be remiss if we did not at least attempt to assess its utility for
explaining their choices.

Theorists frequently argue over whether "occupational
choice" means actual entry into a job or merely an expressed

preference for a given line of work. The problem is pertinent to women since they face many difficulties in actually implementing their preferences. Parents are sometimes unwilling to support them in college, graduate school fellowships are not noticeably abundant for women, married women are not always able to relocate geographically or to secure adequate child care. But these problems operate both during and after college. Thus the preference versus entry controversy does not clarify women's choices—it merely avoids the simple fact that the theories of occupational choice cannot explain women's preferences.

Occupational Choice as Process and Congruence

Two major themes pervade theories of occupational choice. The first is that choosing an occupation is a lengthy *process*, beginning with fantasy choices made in early childhood and lasting until the person completes school and assumes some full time position in late adolescence or early adulthood. The person continually makes tentative choices and considers each one carefully before discarding or retaining it. People are always attempting to bring their choices in line with reality, trying to make a choice that they can actually attain, in terms of their abilities and potential for securing the proper training.

According to Ginzberg and his associates (1951), occupational preferences for males are tentative during the early adolescent years. At first they are determined by interests, then by a need for testing capacities, and eventually by values, including money and indirect satisfactions available from various lines of work. Impending graduation from high school and the problem of deciding among the alternatives of immediate employment, vocational training or college, force the transition stage. At this time the young man takes responsibility for his own future, shifts from subjectiveness to realism, seeks help from other persons, and adopts an instrumental attitude toward work.

The college period is the time for realistic choices. There are three sub-phases: exploration, crystallization and specification, and the time spent in them may vary considerably from person to person. Students in the exploration stage appreciate that they are under a number of conflicting pressures and remain cautious in the face of making a permanent commitment. Usually some tenuous connection is made between choice of major and choice of career. Once they become aware of their propensities and the type of work they prefer to avoid, students make a real choice at least of a general field of work, that is, their choice has crystallized, though further choices may be required. Specification is the culmination of the choice process. It involves specialization and planning within a general occupational field. The Ginzberg study concludes that occupational choice is largely a developmental process which invariably ends in a compromise between internal and external factors, between aspirations and reality and that the process is largely irreversible.

The Ginzberg book has been sharply criticized as being based on "a variety of naively conceived studies which have quizzed children about their occupational choices or asked adults to recall their childhood orientation to work" (Caplow, 1954). Donald E. Super (1953), a psychologist, points out that the Ginzberg volume lightly dismisses the extensive literature developed in the vocational guidance field on the nature and predictive value of inventoried interests. This literature is predicated upon the assumption that interests may be latent or unknown to the person, that the purpose of the guidance counselor is to help individuals recognize their interests and to aid in translating these into occupational choices. What Super fails to note is that Ginzberg and his associates do pay a great deal of attention to interests, but they believe that a person generally knows her or his interests. For them, the final choice is a rational one in which known interests are taken into account.

The *congruence* view suggests that the individual's psychosocial characteristics coincide with the job's requirements. The process of selecting and discarding occupations culminates in the choice of an occupation whose rewards, tasks and requirements are congruent with the person's abilities, values and preferences. Super stresses this second thesis prevalent in the occupational choice research, that vocational choice is the process of developing and implementing a self concept. Through play, school classes, work experience and other activities, people develop thorough knowledge of their capacities and inclinations translating these into an appropriate job choice hospitable to playing one's preferred roles.

Both Ginzberg and Super agree that the choice process inevitably ends in a compromise between individual and social factors, between ability and job requirements, between interests and opportunity, between values and the potential for realizing them. But Ginzberg goes further to suggest that the failure to arrive at a crystallized-specified choice reflects psychological disturbance on the part of the individual. Super (1953) introduces the normative concept of vocational maturity: the extent to which an individual's behavior corresponds to the expected vocational behavior at that age. Vocational maturity is associated with a host of factors including intelligence, parental socio-economic status, family cohesiveness and involvement in extra-curricular activities. Hence Super's concept of vocational maturity and explanations of it are less pejorative towards women than Ginzberg's. Still Super is suggesting that some individuals lack competence in the task of choosing an occupation.

Both the process and congruence approaches have many adherents. The controversies which exist have to do more with refining the two themes rather than refuting them. There is the issue mentioned earlier of whether to define choice as preference for an occupation or actual entry into it. And there is some debate over the degree of rationality attributable to people, whether individuals consciously survey their inclinations and search vigorously for occupations that will satisfy their preferences. In addition, it is unclear whether people really know their own interests or if they need counseling intervention to help discover them.

Perhaps the only seriously competing views concern which characteristics of individuals are the most important for predicting career choice. Variations in values, interests, aptitudes, self concepts, "modal personal orientations" (Holland, 1966), need hierarchies, and a large number of personality traits have all been correlated with variations in occupational choice. The child who likes to work with his hands becomes a carpenter, the independent striving young man chooses business, and girls who want to work with people select nursing or teaching. The resulting correlations are high enough to be statistically significant but low enough to suggest that some mismatching of person and occupation occurs frequently. Part of this mismatching may be explained away because the concept of occupation encompasses a number of jobs, or at least occupation and job are not coterminous. Hence occupations have a good deal of stretch about them, so that one occupation may accommodate a variety of different persons in diverse jobs. Furthermore, most individuals are capable of assuming several different jobs or occupations, and for some there is no clear cut hierarchy of preferences. In spite of this difficulty, researchers remain convinced that if only the right classification of occupational types could be obtained and if the relevant characteristics of individuals could be assayed, the congruence between individual and occupation could be very nearly perfect.

The myth that women choose occupations and pursue careers much like men do dies hard. Holland argues that women do not need a special theory of career development because "men and boys whose initiative and talents are depreciated also have difficulty in obtaining jobs and making a career." Holland makes this argument as if women can be *made* to fit existing occupational choice theories by fiat; but they cannot.

What about women? Most women, even college educated ones, end up choosing occupations which have women as the overwhelming majority of their practitioners. Surely, the interests and inclinations of most women are not so narrowly circumscribed! There is nothing inherently perfect about the fit between femaleness and teaching, nursing or social work, yet women predominate in these fields and college women select them. Furthermore, despite the mismatching between occupation and ability, vocational counselors encourage women to pursue these fields.

Social mobility versus sex role as determinants of choice

Several researchers have been explicit in stating that women's choices do not fit this model. Ginzberg, the originator of the process view, admits that major changes must be made in his theory in order to fit the case of women. Among the very small sample of college women he interviewed, most were uncertain what occupation they would pursue. Strong (1955) found that inventories of vocational interests taken during college were of little use for predicting in which occupations women were actually working several years after graduation. Even for women in a traditionally female field, nursing, the fit between person and occupation can be tenuous (Davis and Olesen, 1963). The most professional nurses, may be the least conforming to the stereotypic nurse—the "bad girls" may be the best nurses (Kruegar, 1968).

Occupational choice does not occur in a vacuum, nor is it a single isolated variable. Occupation is the key factor in setting a man's life style. That choice in turn determines what sort of friends he will have, in what circumstances—in the office or on the factory floor—he will work, whether he will work forty hours a week, promptly forgetting the job once he leaves or if his work will spill over into leisure and family life as well. His choice will affect which neighborhood he lives in, which recreational activities he pursues and what community, church or charitable activities he selects. In short, by choosing an occupation, men are either implicitly or explicitly choosing a life style at least in a socioeconomic sense. Of course, both the job and its associated life style are influenced by his social background and experiences. We might well ask whether men select an occupation and the life style is simply a concomitant, or whether they first aspire to a life style and then choose an occupation as a means to reach it. Delving into these matters, however, obscures the central point that males build their adult lives around their work.

For women, it is much more likely that they are chosen, but do not explicitly choose. So long as the prevailing norms specify that men offer the marriage proposal or the living together and that the social status of the family is linked to the husband's occupation, then the woman's life style is determined by the man who wants her. Females seldom select an occupation for its extrinsic material rewards or for a desired class standing. These are sought through their husband's occupation (Turner, 1964), though women may choose an occupation because it provides an opportunity to meet men of the proper social class (Psathas, 1968).

When they choose a field of work women are generally more attuned to the intrinsic features of the occupation. They seek an occupation which allows them to use their special abilities to work with people rather than things, and one which can be combined with family life. It is sex role, rather than social mobility aspirations, which colors women's choices. All these facts held in 1971 in the American Council on Education Study (Bayer et. al., 1973) as they did in the 1950's when the research efforts on college student values began.

The occupational choices of women are far more circumscribed than those of men. Even college educated women are apt to select predominantly female occupations. Most of the occupations they enter are within the "professional, technical and kindred worker" category of the United States Census. But this category is extremely broad, encompassing occupations as divergent as United States Senator and laboratory technician. Included are occupations which vary as much in prestige as physicist and dental hygienist. There are occupations as powerless as social worker and as omnipotent as supreme court justice. Men are the "real professionals"—the doctors, lawyers, judges and scientists. Women are extraordinarily concentrated in the less prestigious professions of teaching, nursing, social work and librarianship. Sixty percent of all female professionals are in these fields even though men control most of the top administrative posts. Women are more likely than men to occupy the technical positions ancillary to a major profession, as dental hygienist or physical therapist.

The absence of women from the high level professions partially reflects women's lower achievement of graduate level degrees. They are less likely than men to attend graduate or professional school and if they do begin are more likely to drop out (Bisconti and Astin, 1973). But women's lesser educational attainment is only one piece of the puzzle in their limited occupational achievement.

It is the sex-segregated labor force which daily reinforces traditional notions about what work is "suitable for a woman." Fields peopled predominantly by men have come to be seen as manly, masculine or suited to men, and thus virtually taboo to women. Yet other jobs, like secretary, have become synonymous with female.

Males and females are distributed differently throughout the labor force. Women are under-represented in the census category "proprietors, managers, and officials." If they are in these positions, they generally own small retail businesses or have minor administrative posts. The proportion of women managers in manufacturing industries changed not at all in 20 years—it was about six percent both in 1950 and in 1970 (Manpower Report, 1973).

One third of all employed women are secretarial and clerical workers. Only seven percent of male workers are in this category and those who are usually work under special conditions, in the factory, at docks, and railroad stations, where the work is dirty or requires technical knowledge of production processes (Caplow, 1954).

Men predominate in wholesale sales. In retail sales, women sell products that women buy and men handle products that men purchase, or items too expensive, heavy or valuable to be handled by women. Service work may be the occupational category where men and women work together most closely. Yet here women are relegated primarily to restaurants and beauty shops. They are kitchen workers, nurses' aides and charwomen, while men are janitors, hospital attendants and bartenders. Men hold the jobs in protective service—as firemen, guards, sheriffs and policemen.

Women are almost totally absent from farm owners and managers and from the relatively high paying blue collar occupations of craftsmen and foremen. While equal proportions of male and female workers are factory operatives, the two sexes do not mingle freely on the job. In each industry or individual factory, men and women are assigned different tasks in the division of labor. At the bottom of the occupational ladder, women form the bulk of the domestic workers while the "laborer" category is almost exclusively male.

In sum, the American labor force is amazingly segregated by sex, so much so that nearly 70 percent of women workers would have to change occupations if men and women were to work together side by side in equivalent jobs (Gross, 1968). The same objective (equalizing the distribution of men and women in the occupational structure) could be accomplished by men entering women's fields, but so far they have been reluctant to do so. Occupations which were predominantly female in 1900 were still predominantly female in 1970. The 1970 Census statistics show clearly that there has been no lessening of sexual barriers. Women have entered some occupations in greater numbers than before. But they have entered fields in which they were originally so scarce that they do not change the sex ratio or they have taken up jobs in fields that are growing so rapidly that their strength is countered by an increase in male workers as well.

How can we account for this persistent sex typing of occupations? Two explanations are common: one is that women choose those occupations which fit most easily with their motherhood-family-domestic responsibilities and are an extension of women's nurturing, helping orientation. The second is that occupational structure reflects family structure, so that women avoid positions which place them in competition with men or require initiating action. They work as the supervised, in positions of subservience to men. Women, more attuned to personal and affectional relationships forego situations requiring skills for abstraction or leadership roles.

These arguments fit the supply side of the equation that women enter only a limited number of occupations because they have been socialized to prefer them. Oppenheimer (1968) adds a new emphasis when she points to the demand factor. Most employers are male—they believe that women have certain characteristics, such as manual dexterity, patience for routine and sex appeal, which presumably endow them with ability to perform well in certain fields. In addition, women are rarely hired where on-the-job training is essential since employers are reluctant to invest in a woman—they argue that she may not stay very long. Employers fear the sexuality element in mixed work groups and they shun women supervisors like the plague. As a result of all this, they sex-label jobs and advertise, recruit and hire women accordingly. Stressing either the supply factor of women's preferences or the demand factor of men's employment practices makes little difference for our purposes. Both explanations point clearly to the supremacy of sex role over individual inclination and ability in explaining women's career choices.

Women's Lives and Their Career Choices

Of course, the work careers of women are not normally continuous. Mature women work intermittently, leaving the labor force after the birth of the first child, and returning again for many reasons. Women seek work after divorce breaks one household into two, in times of family financial emergencies, or to help finance their children's college education. Financial need is the reason women in their mid-years most often give for returning to paid employment. In fact, a disproportionate share of the female labor force is composed of widows, divorcees and separated women who are the sole support of dependent children, and married women whose husbands' incomes are below the poverty line (Waldman and Gover, 1972).

Nonetheless many researchers and employers continue to assume that women work for frivolous reasons—for luxuries or to escape boredom at home—and that they are mostly secondary breadwinners. Since women are usually confined to the location of their husband's work, and since women must desert the labor force when family demands are pressing, women often cannot pursue occupations which require continuous work, or whole-hearted devotion to the exclusion of other demands on their time. But they gain no relief from labor. Far from having more leisure than men, working women have less; women average between one and two hours less leisure each day (Hedges and Barnett, 1972).

Instead of recognizing women's diverse interests and abilities or contemplating how early women learn to assume family responsibility, or considering the benefits to families (both husband and wives) of part-time work, male observers stress the deficiency attached to such flexible strategies. Instead of valuing contributions to family, community and society, they ridicule volunteer work as superficial, as *non-gainful* employment. Instead of adapting higher level professions to account for women's family work, they rationalize and denigrate the jobs women fill. Instead of defining medicine as a nurturing occupation suitable to women, as do the Soviets, Americans see doctors as authority figures and technical specialists—and hence as male. Such reasoning is evident even in a sociologist's view:

> Given the intermittent character of female employment, a woman's occupation must be one in which employment is typically by short term, in which the gain in skill achieved by continuous experience is slight, in which interchangeability is very high, and in which the loss of skill during long periods of inactivity is relatively small. Note how closely the occupations of elementary teacher, nurse, librarian, shop clerk, typist, sewing machine operator, and waitress conform to these criteria (Caplow, 1954, p. 245).

Yet, it has been demonstrated that within the same occupations women have no higher turnover or absenteeism rates than men do (U.S. Department of Labor, 1969). Many of the occupations Caplow lists are not markedly different from those in which men are concentrated—high school teacher, waiter, chef—and it is questionable whether the work tasks are distinct. Cross-cultural ironies abound to contradict such sex-typing. Ruth Useem, (personal communication) tells about the high percentage of women among chemists because they can cook!

Sex role learning begins at birth and is mainly unconscious. By the time they enter college, women perceive that family and motherhood can limit their occupational plans. Women's potential aspirations are deflected in advance so that, even as young girls, they seldom think of themselves as physicians or lawyers or physicists. Lenore Harmon (1971) asked college freshmen women to check all the occupations from a comprehensive list which they had ever considered entering. Less than ten percent had ever thought of such highly visible occupations as dentist, pilot, pharmacist or school principal. Other occupations which boys commonly think of, but less than ten percent of these women ever considered, were photographer, reporter, mathematician, surgeon, and income tax accountant.

The early inculcation of lower aspirations for women shows among the college graduates Alice Rossi surveyed. Four out of five respondents actually admired winners of scientific, scholarly or artistic awards. When asked in what way they would personally like to be successful, the most frequent answers were to be the mother of several accomplished children or to be the wife of a prominent man. Less than seven percent of this group were pioneers—women who had long range career goals in the predominantly masculine fields of science, business management, administration, medicine, law, engineering, architecture, dentistry or economics (Rossi, 1965). Cynthia Epstein hypothesizes that "the socialization process works on the woman in such a way that she often decides against a career without actually testing reality. . . . She anticipates consequences and accepts limitations or defeat which may not be inevitable in her case" (Epstein, 1970, p. 76).

During college, the sorting of the sexes into fields is striking. While both are likely to change their preferences between freshman and senior year of college, women are pulled toward "women's" fields and men toward "men's" fields. Women tend to major in education, social science or the humanities. Males take the majority of degrees granted in mathematics, the natural sciences and philosophy. Just as home economics is 98 percent female, engineering is 98 percent male. Biology is one of the few fields with roughly equal percentages of male and female undergraduate majors (Davis, 1965). Partly as a consequence of this differential recruitment to fields, annual college graduations present men and women trained for very different occupations.

Women college graduates are more often employed as teachers than anything else. A 1964 survey of the graduating class of 1957 revealed that 60 percent of those who had worked did so in teaching. Nursing and secretarial work were the next two most frequent occupations (Women's Bureau, Department of Labor, 1966). In the seven year interval between graduation and the time of the survey, only 15 percent had obtained a master's degree, and of those who did, 43 percent took a degree in education, nine percent in English and eight percent in sociology or social work. So the drift toward feminine fields of study persists even among those who pursue advanced work in graduate school.

Women's sorting and selecting of fields mirrors the kinds of values and interests they develop in growing up female. Men prefer occupations which allow freedom from close supervision, while women are more intent on being original and creative in their work. The status concerns of men show up in preference for occupations which offer an opportunity to make money; women are more interested in an occupation which can be easily combined with family duties. Women are more oriented toward working in an occupation which allows helping others and they prefer working with people rather than alone or with "things" (Rosenberg, 1957; Epstein, 1970). But these are comparative differences, not absolute ones. Alongside these value differences, women who are strongly interested in pursuing a career resemble males in their work values. Recent studies of the femininity-masculinity dimension of personality (M-F) reveal great overlap between men's and women's scores; career-oriented women even in humanities and fine arts resemble men in M-F measures and are quite unlike domestically-oriented women (Rand, 1971). Furthermore, this overlap between male and female personality characteristics has been growing (Vincent, 1966).

The winds of change in work and life values are encouraging. We are witnessing the increasing overlap not only in personalities of women and men but also in attitudes and aspirations. In their longitudinal study of college students, Bayer and associates (1973) report that in 1967 more than half the sample agreed that activities of married women should be confined to home and family whereas in 1971, about one quarter endorsed this view. At the same time, a shift in life objectives has been occurring, so that students are less concerned with attaining status, recognition or financial success.

Despite these trends, to affect women's career aspirations requires fundamental changes in socialization and in educational and occupational opportunities.

The next three chapters go beyond mere description of career development during college. We present our efforts to understand the complexity of women's choices. By encompassing a multi-dimensional view of occupation, field choices are scrutinized to see whether women, like men, crystallize and narrow their preferences. We look for possible congruence between field preferences and personal values, and try to ascertain what factors explain career-oriented life style aspirations. We will highlight some special features of women who choose male-dominated fields, indicate the important influence of role models in women's career aspirations, and put a fresh face on career aspirers—they emerge as different but not deviant; their backgrounds show a richness in offering options and encouragement to pursue careers.

7 How Women Choose an Occupation

All through their lives, women make choices and evidence behavior in a somewhat special way, different enough from men but not totally. The values women apply in living constantly reflect their "feminine" socialization, their hesitancy to make long-range plans, their fear of setting independent goals, their urge to stay involved with people and in service, above all their orientation toward family and homemaking.

Yet educated women in particular train for occupations, move into the work force, and even seek advanced professional training as if they were men. They follow the pattern that colleges encourage: be practical, prepare for earning a living, choose something interesting to work at and try to be successful.

Integrating the two messages is far from easy. It is difficult even for educated women to implement all these aims. Why so difficult? Mainly because both the educational and work worlds are organized to reflect men's lives and masculine goals. In pursuing, first, higher education and, next, a profession, women face constant dilemmas.

In most universities, education for women will ideally provide "a minor marketable skill so they can be secondary earners until the babies come, with enough liberal arts so they can 'enrich' their children's lives and not disgrace themselves in front of the husband's business associates . . ." (Scott, 1971). The woman is educated as Veblen believed to be "useless and expensive" and hence "valuable as evidence of pecuniary strength" (Veblen, 1899).

If the college woman tries to refute such prevailing goals she finds no help from textbooks, professors or male classmates. She discovers quickly that all the great people in western civilization were men, that science, technology, psychology, sociology, poetry and art were all developed and shaped by men, If she dares to ask about accomplishments of women, she is told: "Yes, there are exceptions." At that point, a few great women are named: Marie Curie, George Eliot, Jane Austin. . . . As the list peters out the explanation begins, the explanation that, of course few women ever achieve greatness.

After that argument, the woman who persists in pursuit of a profession begins to sense that she is the proverbial wolf in sheep's clothing—she is female trying to be male, trying to be "like them," to do "what they do." Neither her teachers nor her classmates appreciate this because now the woman is "no longer feminine." Yet if she fails to subscribe to the predominantly male views about work and career, she is "unprofessional."

Now, imagine that our female careerist has long forgotten the childish couplet about occupation:

Rich man, poor man, beggar man, thief,
Doctor, lawyer, Indian chief. . . .

Or else believe that she took it as her own. And suppose that she can overlook the confused expectations about her goals. She then notices that the very language of the academy (and later of the work world) is full of masculinities; from pronouns to adjectives to verbs, the language abounds in male conceptions of professionals and of performance. In classrooms the talk is of the contributions to "mankind" by "him," by "his" work. In faculty meetings, the talk is of promoting "outstanding men" and of "hiring a guy who can do great work." And everywhere, the talk is of "mastering the task," "getting to the top," "being aggressive, strong, dominant, competitive."

Amidst all these conditions, women try to choose a field of work, to shape a life. When we look at the college women whom we studied with these conditions in mind, their specific ways of choosing an occupation become more understandable.

We begin by asking whether these women do show a narrowing of occupational choices, from very general fields to more specific types of work. And we find no neat pattern at all; rather, shifting and changing occupational preferences predominate. Then we check to see whether the frequent changing involves a search for congruence between one's work values and a field choice. There seems to be a strong sex-tied pattern of choice rather than the fitting of an occupation to the woman's ideas about desirable work. Since neither of these approaches clarify occupational choices, we turn to a different dimension, more applicable for women— the preference for male-dominated occupations. Instead of trying to explain all the women's choices, we can more carefully analyze distinctions between the pioneers who venture into "men's work" and the conventional women who prefer "women's work."

Do Women Narrow Their Choices?

The first result is the pervasive changeability among the study group—their occupational preferences shift frequently. Perhaps the frequency of change we discovered is an artifact of the methods employed. The women were repeatedly questioned about their post-college plans and they were asked to describe the occupation in detail. Students may have felt pressured to write down something, anything, in the blank merely to get finished with the task. However, the count of changes includes only those instances where a real change occurred; it does not emcompass minor alterations in content of the women's responses. For example, a student who wrote journalism one year, and newspaper or magazine writing the next, was not counted as a changer, while one who said textile research at one point and technical writing about textiles the next was.

Interviews with the students confirm their changeability. Nearly all these women are talented students making good grades at a rather selective university. Fields such as the social sciences and the humanities in which many of the students majored open a variety of work options. Ever alert to new opportunities, students respond by considering many different varieties of work. This is as true for career-oriented students as for those who are not oriented toward a career. Many of the dramatic shifts in occupational choice are recorded at the same time that students show a change in their major field of study. In the interviews, the most frequent reason given for changing major, particularly in the fall of the junior year, is that an occupational goal was incompatible with the old major.

If the great amount of changing that occurs is not obviously an artifact of the methods employed, then a closer look at the nature of the changes is in order. Recall from the last chapter the view that in the reality phase, the person chooses broad fields and then narrows down to a crystallized, specified choice. An alternative view is that the person chooses a general field or even a specific occupation, and "tries on" the anticipated occupational role. She or he either retains that choice or rejects it, choosing a new field all over again. In the first view, changes in choice during the college years involve only progressive crystallization; in the second, choice is much more open-ended and manifest in marked shifts or abrupt changes in preferences. Both views have their adherents and both correspond to reality for some persons.

In this study the questionnaires were systematically

reviewed to characterize the pattern of changing each individual evidenced over the four time periods. The figures in Table 7-1 then refer to as many as three changes in responses. The number of non-changers given here includes students who listed the same occupation as seniors that they had given as freshmen, in spite of a different choice in the intervening years.

Table 7-1. Patterns of Change in Occupational Choice

Pattern	Percent
No change	9
Progressive narrowing	21
Change within same general field	22
Change to another field	39
Choice becomes less specific	9
Total	100%

Roughly one fifth of the students exhibit the pattern of selecting a field and progressively narrowing the alternatives within it. For example one student wrote "definitely math" as a sophomore, "definitely math" as a junior and "teach high-school math" in her senior year. Many students fit this style of picking a discipline, usually their major, and eventually select teaching as the best way to implement their desire to work in that field. Another example of the progressive narrowing pattern is "biology," "biological research" and "working in a pharmaceutical company, doing research."

Another one fifth of the students keep vacillating within a general field. Two examples are "department store buyer," "buyer," "fashion co-ordinator"; and "technical writing in chemistry or biology," "advertising-graphic work," "advertising/will begin as a secretary," "advertising/copy or technical writing." These women remain crystallized on a general field, but undergo repeated specifications.

Nearly two fifths of the sample experience dramatic shifts in their choice, changing from one field to another. Most of these occur at sophomore or junior year, and further changes ordinarily involve progressive narrowing within the new field. One student considered "government work" in her freshman year, "government work in the Justice Department" as a sophomore and in her junior year shifted to "social work." Another wrote "teaching history," "historical research," "law or teaching," and at last "corporation lawyer." One student considered three separate fields; her responses were "medicine," "writing," "I don't know," and "law."

Finally, a small group of students reverse the narrowing pattern by originally indicating a crystallized, specified choice and then moving, during their later years of college, to a broader, less specific field. Examples include someone who stated "economic statistician" and later simply "economics," or a girl who at one point suggested "either journalism or advertising," but as a senior said "I don't know."

This somewhat conservative measure of change shows then that just over half the class members follow the pattern Ginzberg and his associates (1951) predicted. Those who undergo no definite change, those who exhibit the progressive narrowing pattern and those who shift occupations within the same general field may be construed as proceeding in a relatively orderly manner to sift out their options. The other half of the class make repeated, dramatic shifts in their choices, or become less definitive. Several respondents did not list the same occupation more than once. All the students were indecisive and wavering at some time during college. Obviously if one focuses on only the last years of college, most students express the Ginzberg pattern. But the sophomore year is the year for going out on a limb, for trying new alternatives. After that time most students remain crystallized on the same field, though not too many have specified a particular job.

Students who major in the applied fields—home economics, business studies, technical writing—are by virtue of the emphasis of course content led to select specific vocations.

The textiles and retailing option directs students toward being department-store buyers; the foods and nutrition specialty points to being a nutritionist or dietician; business-studies students are preparing to be either secretaries or teachers. Yet these women are little more certain about their occupational preferences or the probability of pursuing them than students in the non-vocationally specific liberal arts fields.

Do Occupational Choices Match Work Values?

Repeated change is the most characteristic feature of women's choices during college, especially during the first two years. To be sure, the theories of occupational choice predict that change will occur, with the end result that students select an occupation that is congruent with their abilities, interests and values. Rosenberg (1957) showed that students tend to change their occupational choices to conform with their values far more frequently than they change their values to conform with an occupational choice. So some of the changing that college women exhibit may represent an attempt to bring their choices in line with the values they hold. But the frequency and extent of change among the study class are sufficiently marked to suggest either that their values are also subject to wide, swinging vacillations *or* that women students have a rather difficult time implementing their values. The first assumption can be tested empirically.

On each administration of the questionnaire, students were asked: "How important do you think the following features of an occupation have been or will be in influencing your choice of a field of work?" The five response categories ranged from "completely unimportant" to "very important." Table 7-2 shows the nine work features, the percent of the study class who considered each feature quite or very important in freshman and senior year, and the ranking of the work values obtained by ordering them according to the percent who considered them important in each year.

Table 7-2. Work Features Rated Important

Work feature	Senior responses		Freshman responses	
	Percent quite or very important	Rank order	Percent quite or very important	Rank order
Allows use of special abilities	87	1	84	1
Involves work with people rather than alone or with things	73	2	83	2
Allows combining career and good family life	72	3	64	4
Provides freedom from close supervision	63	4	34	7
Provides stable, secure future	53	5	69	3
Has prospects of high income	51	6	45	6
Involves helping others	49	7	53	5
Occupation has high prestige	18	8	7	9
Suits parents' idea of success	14	9	9	8

The Spearman rank order correlation between senior and freshman responses is $r_s = +.833$.

The remarkable fact is the stability of students' evaluations of various work features between the first and last years of college. Altogether an average of 50 percent of the students rate the work features important as freshmen; as seniors 53 percent do so. The percentage rating on the individual items fluctuates somewhat, especially for the moderately valued work features, yet the rank ordering remains fairly consistent.

As freshmen, the women are interested in an occupation that provides a stable, secure feature and allows helping others, but these values lose in importance. The students are originally unconcerned about being free from close supervision; they become so by senior year. This is the only work value that gains significantly in importance over the four years, and "stable, secure future" is the only one that loses significantly.

The constancy with which students evaluate the features that are high in importance and those that are low in importance is noteworthy. "Has prospects of high income" remains steadily in sixth place, with about half the students valuing this characteristic highly. Similarly, the low emphasis women place on high status is seen in that "occupation has high prestige" and "suits parents' ideas of success" are the least preferred work characteristics in both freshmen and senior years. Though one might question whether women are rejecting success or their parents' views on the matter, these findings are consistent with the general view that sex-role inculcation leads women to forego prestige and status strivings in their own choice of occupation.

"Allows use of special abilities" is a work value men and women frequently share. Such an emphasis is especially prevalent at a university that is very expensive to attend and that stresses technological training. But other concerns are more crucial for women, as seen in the other two top ranked values: women are socialized to prefer working with people rather than engaging in solitary pursuits or manipulating machinery and objects; combining a career and a good family life are essential as well.

Decidedly feminine in their values, the class as a whole retains the same preferences as seniors that they held as freshmen. In addition, the individual students are reasonably consistent. Hence very little of the dramatic changes in occupational choices can be attributed to alterations in work values. With notable exceptions, women's values remain firm, and they obviously have difficulty in sorting through and finding occupations that conform with their values. How this works out will be seen in the next section, where students who choose female-dominated occupations are compared with those who opt for male-dominated fields.

The Choice of Male-Dominated Occupations

Researchers have used several schemes for dividing occupations into categories. Holland (1959, 1962), for example, proposed six major types of work environments: Motoric-Realistic (farmers, truck drivers); Intellectual (chemists, biologists); Social-Supportive (teachers, social workers); Conventional-Conforming (bookkeepers, bank tellers); Persuasive-Enterprising (salesmen, politicians); Esthetic-Artistic (musicians, artists). James Davis (1965) divided the career choices of undergraduate students into ten categories including the physical sciences, the biological sciences, the social sciences, humanities and fine arts, education, engineering, medicine, law, other professional fields and business. Virtually no researchers have intended to type occupations according to their composition by sex, yet most of the classifications just given *are* sex-typed, with men predominating in certain fields and women very prevalent in others.

In her book *Women's Place*, Cynthia Epstein (1970) offers the thesis that women are the "wrong" sex, especially in the sciences, with the consequence that males react to women as females rather than as colleagues. She also points to the major impediments facing the wrong sex, hypothesizing that "the low percentage of women in professional life was probably . . . a reflection of the fact that those who ultimately chose a profession did so idiosyncratically, rather than through a sequence of introduction, training and assumption of career" (Epstein, 1970, p. 29). For women, the routes to professional careers are haphazard, accidental and not positively sanctioned.

We lack understanding of the process by which a young woman finds and enters a work role reasonably congruent with her self-concept. Not everyone succeeds in making such a link before graduation. A few clues from the theoretical literature and a thorough analysis of the current findings show that women who choose atypical or male-dominated occupations do not differ appreciably in the process of making a choice, yet they do differ greatly in the *content of the influences* on their choice. Work values, occupational role models, and personal work experience comprise the major factors differentiating atypical from typical choosers. Let us consider these in closer detail.

We classified occupations as atypical for women in the following way: Women constituted at least one third of the adult labor force, according to the 1960 Census. If they were distributed in the labor force in the same proportion as men, each occupation would have the same make-up by sex—approximately two-thirds male and one-third female. Obviously this was not the case. Hence, any occupation with less than one-third women was termed male-dominated, or atypical for women. All others were judged typical.

By this scheme, 34 women made masculine choices as seniors: lawyer, college professor, and biological, chemical, or psychological researcher are the most frequent atypical choices. Miscellaneous male-dominated selections include personnel management, economist and statistician. High-school teaching, social work, journalism, consumer economics, translator, dietician, executive secretary and buyer were all classified as feminine or typical women's fields.

The results indicate an association between major field of study and the choice of male-dominated occupations (Table 7-3). Students in the natural sciences are most likely to select an atypical occupation; those who do not are primarily future teachers or plan to work as laboratory technicians in the pharmaceutical industry. Women in the social sciences and the humanities are almost equally likely to choose female or male-dominated jobs. Majors in the applied fields are very unlikely to choose a masculine job, primarily because nearly all these students are in home economics or business studies, training to be secretaries, dieticians or teachers.

Table 7-3. Major Field and Atypicality of
Occupational Choice for Seniors

Major Field	N	Percent choosing male-dominated occupation
Natural sciences	13	62
Humanities	20	50
Social sciences	18	56
Applied fields	36	17
Total	87	39%

The university experience apparently does not lure women into pioneering fields. There are no marked gains in the number of students preferring male-dominated occupations. The school's input shows up primarily through the opportunity for students to sample among various majors. Since these are bright, capable students who chose this professionally oriented school, they are rather receptive to various opportunities. Looking at the choices made all four years, 65 percent choose a male-dominated job at least once. But 85 percent indicate a traditional choice at least once. So sex-typing prevails, with women more likely to consider and eventually settle on feminine occupations rather than masculine ones.

Both typical and atypical choosers are about equally likely to postpone or change their occupational choice, and to feel uncertain about whether they will actually pursue it. The two groups do exhibit slightly different patterns of change. The typical choosers are more likely to exhibit no change at all, or to move from a detailed, specific choice to stating only a vague field of work. The women who choose male-dominated occupations more often follow the pattern of stating a general field and then narrowing to a specific occupation, or of changing choices within a particular field.

The work values students bring with them and maintain through the four years of school noticeably distinguish the masculine from the feminine choosers. Table 7-4 shows that there are only three work features on which the judgment of the two groups coincide. They both favor an occupation that can be combined with family life, and are only moderately interested in a stable, secure future. Both groups downgrade the notion of high prestige as an occupational feature. On the remaining items the students' preferences clearly diverge, with the atypical choosers selecting the people-oriented aspects of work. Women who prefer male-dominated occupations more often prefer high income; they insist on being free from close supervision; and they are adamant about wanting to use their special abilities. Those who choose female occupations express the more traditional feminine values of working with people rather than things, helping others and suiting their parents' ideas of success.

Table 7-4. Atypicality of Occupational Choice and Work Values

Work feature	Atypical choosers — Percent quite or very important	Typical choosers — Percent quite or very important
Allows use of special abilities	100	79
Allows combining career with good family life	71	73
Provides freedom from close supervision	71	58
Has prospects of high income	65	42
Provides stable, secure future	56	52
Occupation has high prestige	18	17
Involves work with people rather than alone or with things	62	81
Involves helping others	44	54
Suits parents' ideas of success	6	19

One further value separates the masculine from the feminine choosers. Students are unlikely to seek a male-dominated occupation unless they are also strongly career-oriented. Among the career aspirers, 59 percent choose male-dominated while 41 percent choose female-dominated fields. And of those women who are not career aspirers, a sizeable 78 percent choose typical women's occupations while only 22 percent seek atypical fields. Those few non-careerists who do select male-dominated occupations may be quite unrealistic. For example, one student said her choice is "to be a consultant and adviser in a large company in the fashion world, coordinating sales, advertising and market research." When asked if she knew anyone who now holds that sort of job she replied, "No, really it is just something that I conjured up in my mind as the ideal situation for me." Perhaps such women mean that they are really not interested in working, but if they do, it will have to be a desirable and prestigious job.

The other "contrary" pattern is somewhat more understandable. It includes women interested in a career for themselves but who plan to work in a typically feminine field. About one in five students display this pattern. Few of these women plan to work while their children are very young, but they consider work an important part of their lives. When we asked one of these students if she wants to teach after having a family she replied:

> As soon as I got them into school I would. Right now I can't see myself just making beds and doing dishes. But I know I like to teach seniors in high school . . . I don't think I want more than two children because you can't support more than that well. As soon as they are six years old I will work because I just won't be satisfied sitting around the house. I have to be around people and it would add to the income so I could help in two ways.

Apparently working is seen by this student as a way to escape boredom and to earn money. Most of the career salient, typical choosers plan to be teachers or social workers. These choices are ones that the students believe can be combined with marriage. They also reflect a strong desire to serve society.

Work Experience and Occupational Choice

Slocum found in 1956 that high school and college women

saw work experience as the single most frequent source of influence on the occupations they chose. Our data also plainly show that work experience affects students' occupational decisions in several important ways. Some of the students planning to be department store buyers decided against that option after serving an internship in that field. Others reported deciding against various types of work after looking more closely at the occupation. The students' limited exploration of various occupations through course work was also helpful in orienting them. Change in major frequently occurred after sampling the work possibilities via course content, although courses and term projects were secondary sources of occupational knowledge.

More importantly, the amount of work experience significantly differentiates between women who choose male-dominated occupations and those who select female-dominated occupations. Sixty-two percent of the former group had held four or more jobs compared with only 34 percent of the latter. Women who choose masculine fields also had a *greater variety* of work experience: 71 percent had held three or more different jobs. Only 38 percent of the typical choosers had worked at three separate positions. The greater amount and variety of work experience exposes students to a broader view of the composition of the labor force. Those who choose atypical fields must have a more thorough knowledge of the requirements of various lines of work. Students who have more work experience perhaps can better appreciate their own competencies and preferences.

We wondered whether the actual jobs students experienced might be tied to the type of occupation they select. The atypical choosers are slightly more likely to have worked in jobs related to their senior occupational preference. The most frequent jobs students held were camp counsellor, secretary, salesgirl, and assistant in father's business. Teaching, swimming, dancing or music occurred often, as did library, hospital, and department-store work. By senior year some women had technical experience in fields connected with their college major, such as hospital and laboratory technician, technical writing, social work, and assisting with psychology experiments. Half the class members were privileged in this respect. Working in entry jobs similar to the one's preferred occupation is an important aid in clarifying occupational plans.

Work experience is crucial in helping students to decide on a particular line of work in another way. Sixty-nine percent of those students who were very certain they would actually pursue their chosen occupation had held four or more jobs. Less than half of the students who were fairly certain or undecided had that much work experience. Similarly, two thirds of the women who were very decided haó held one or more jobs related to their preferred occupation. Less than one third of the students who had not yet chosen an occupation as seniors had any job related to their tentative occupational choice. The possibility for narrowing down a field choice through work experience, and especially in a related field, seems to encourage choice of an atypical occupation. Or perhaps a mutual reinforcement occurs so that women attracted to male-dominated occupations show more initiative in testing out their interests through job experience.

The evidence then is clear: work experience in a variety of jobs enhances the probability that students will crystallize their occupational choices and that they will select male-dominated occupations. One out of every two students prefers an occupation related to a job she has held. Work experience enables women to match their own preferences and abilities with the job requirements, and sometimes work experience places women in contact with role models who can influence their choice.

Who Influences the Atypical Chooser?

On each questionnaire students were asked to indicate from a list which person had most influenced their choice of occupation. If they were undecided about their occupational choice, that is, did not feel they had chosen an occupation, they were asked to indicate which person they expected to influence their choice. Responses were classified into three categories: (1) family, primarily mother or father, and husband; (2) occupational role models who were college teachers or persons in the occupation chosen; and (3) myself or no one. Women who choose male-dominated fields are twice as likely as the girls who choose female-dominated jobs to say that occupational role models had been the major source of influence on their choice. Women choosing typical fields more often say that their parents, usually their mother, was the important influencer. The several undecided women who were considering feminine occupations tend to say that they expect their husband (or future husband) to heavily influence their choice.

The senior interviews amplify these findings. Many students could not give a detailed retrospective account of their occupational decision-making and we did not press hard for them to do so. What is striking about their response is that the women choosing male-dominated fields could give richer descriptions of how they settled on a particular occupation than the other students. These women had more often been impressed by occupational role models; either college teachers had taken a personal interest in them and their work or they already knew persons in the occupation they planned to pursue. More importantly, they had received inputs from several sources rather than just one person. Consider the following exchange between the interviewer and a student who planned to do college teaching and research in chemistry:

Student: I guess my interest in chemistry originally stems from my father and my family. Our family is educationally oriented. My sister, my mother and my father are teachers. I was originally going to go for high-school teaching. But I felt that teaching high school would not allow for the more intricate aspects of chemistry, and I wanted to do research as well as teach. I decided to go more for college teaching.

Interviewer: Other than your family, do you know of other particular persons who might have influenced you?

Student: I would say my research adviser for the past two semesters. I consider him one of the few people who is really interested in other people. I guess in a way I am trying to copy him.

Interviewer: What would you want to copy about him?

Student: Just his interest in people. I feel that because of his vocation he can pursue both his interest in science and his interest in people, whereas out in industry it is a great deal more difficult.

Another student's comments illustrate the way in which those with atypical preferences frequently get to know their college professors as friends and work closely with them on a project. When asked what persons had influenced her choice of psychological research, she replied:

Dr. S is really quite a guy. He is informal and never condescending and yet you know he knows so much more than you do. And I guess Bob M., who is temporary head of the computer department. I got to know him both on an academic and a social level. We talk a lot about computers and the fact that I am interested in that. And now the work I am doing with Dr. W. It turns out that the experiment I did for him last year on the way kids solve math problems is a perfect continuation of his research. He analyzed my data in relation to his data-processing model and it is fixed and we are publishing. All these big things are happening.

Occupational role models are also important because they aid the student in clarifying and realizing her plans. One student planning to do biological research in industry was asked if she knew anyone already employed in that kind of work. Her reply:

Yes, a couple of my friends in biology who work in different companies. I just sit down and talk to them and become familiar with what people do. I learn about the attitudes of the companies, how they treat people. . . . One of my teachers had worked in industry before. He teaches you the very practical kind of stuff you will need to know, not just a classical education. When I get a job I won't have to say, I never learned any of this and you are going to have to teach me from the beginning.

The masculine choosers have more extensive contacts with people outside their immediate family than do typical choosers. These contacts are sufficiently rare and unusual that some women feel dramatically influenced to enter that particular occupation. By contrast, the women who select female-dominated occupations more often feel influenced by persons within their immediate family. Their descriptions of the choice process are less enthusiastic and more matter-of-fact. A business major, asked how she decided to become a teacher, replied:

I don't know. I just kind of fell into it. I transferred out of history because I wanted something more practical. My mother has always wanted me to take the teaching option for the security of it. I thought, well it is not going to take too many electives, so I may as well go into education and I will have something behind me if I want to get married. Then I can always go back into teaching.

Although the women with typical occupations are generally less explicit about the routes to their particular job, they too sometimes feel aided by occupational role models:

Mrs. W. gave me the first organized impression I had of teaching and she gave me more facts. After I had her for a while, she seemed a very nice teacher and a very good teacher, and she would mention things like hours and the working conditions, and I guess it was part attitude and part facts that I got from her that made me decide to teach, too.

More often these students drift into a field because it is convenient or expected:

I guess you have to have something to fall back on and teaching is such a great profession for that. You can never tell what the future is going to hold for you. One reason why I went into teaching . . . my father always mentioned it, my step-mother and my mother and my step-father. Since they knew how fantastic I was with kids they kept pressuring me toward this. I decided that I really want to teach.

Theories of Occupational Choice . . . Again

In this chapter, we reviewed our findings about occupational choice and especially highlighted some differences between women who prefer male-dominated and those who prefer female-dominated fields. In the next chapter, we shall give a more elaborate interpretation of the influence of role models on the larger matter of career orientation.

Although many in our study select masculine career fields, the majority do not. They slip quietly into traditional feminine pursuits. In spite of the professional-vocational-masculine emphasis at this university, sex role predominates in the values women hold and in the occupations they choose. The general experience of college does little to aid women in extricating their occupational plans from sex-role concerns. The liberal-arts fields do not translate directly into a specific occupation. Students in vocationally specific fields are also in traditional women's fields.

Occupational choice theories were framed for men. The pivotal notion is that individuals have free rein to follow their inclinations. The theories do not recognize the major limitations placed on women by their early socialization and by the sex-structuring of the labor force, with the result that women perceive only a narrow range of alternatives. The import of sex role is highlighted implicitly in the stress on social mobility aspirations among men and the latent assumption that women are unlikely to be serious about work so that their choice patterns do not matter. This last assumption is erroneous, since we have demonstrated that the degree of career salience and even the interest in male fields among women varies enormously.

Sex role is far more important for women in that the numerous contingencies prevent women from settling promptly on a particular vocation. And the occupational choice theorists have been unwilling to recognize that even bright, adept, socially mature individuals have difficulty crystallizing a particular choice. What is needed is more attention to the way in which women seek to mesh occupational roles with their other concerns. For women, the exact occupation may be less important than how much work, at which times in life and with what kind of involvement. Choice of occupation becomes meaningful only as part of the plan for adult life after college.

8 Women Use Role Models for Adult Life

Women are in a movement of what Luria (1972) calls "rising expectations." There is little doubt about that. Women want the good life just as everyone these days seems to want it. But the woman's version is not so much a longing for material things to aid the family as it once was; in fact, it is not so totally family-centered as before. There is more sense, especially among the educated, for a need for self-fulfillment, for an interesting and challenging life. For increasingly more women, these goals seem embodied in higher education and in professional careers. But American women, like their counterparts in other countries, now pursue such goals by shedding little and adding much—they take on the "double life" of home and work (Neugarten, 1972).

How do women learn to take on so much? When they opt to hold a job and run a household, the decision can mean a fuller life, but it is also a more difficult one. The employed mother gives up some leisure time, because she has a longer day of work and household chores than does her husband (Walker, 1972; Szalai, 1972).

As in the socialization process generally, people learn partly by observing others for clues about their own behavior. Harley (1972) suggests that when more than half the adult women are employed outside the home, a figure we are rapidly approaching, this provides a prescription for younger women to follow. At this "tipping point" of 50 percent, the role of working woman, or employed mother, becomes commonplace; but more than that, it serves as a model to move even more women into the work world.

This role-modeling process need not be unconscious or covert. Young people often recognize and express their desire for new experiences and for exposure to various people from whom they can learn. A recent survey of graduating seniors at Stanford revealed this kind of awareness (Stanford Committee, 1972). Nearly one third of the students studied thought academic advisers had some effect on their occupational plans. These advisers were considered most influential as role models. Students frequently indicated that the "adviser acted as a positive example" of an individual in the field, but indicated that advisers could also serve as negative examples of people in the field. Advisers were equally important as role models for men and women students, even though most of these faculty members were males. "College is a place for socializing expectations for marriage, work and self-actualization for women as well as for men. People do not learn this by rote or contagion. The juniors watch the seniors; and the sophomores watch the juniors watching the seniors, and everyone watches the professors" (Luria, 1972, p. 32).

It is this process of seeking influences and being influenced that we explored in the college women whom we studied over four years. Our hunch was that career-aspiring women may be exposed to different influences from the non-career oriented.* We suspected that family, friends, teachers and work colleagues might exert some effect on the women's willingness to seek a career. While we could not directly observe such an influence process, we assumed that the students themselves might perceive certain people as influential. We propose that more goes on than mere learning of a work role. Instead, we provide evidence that women benefit from role models who demonstrate a total life style.

Using the twin concepts of reference group and role model, in this chapter, we explore the differences in background between career and non-career aspirers, and we find that some of the sources of influences do indeed differ. Both categories of women often share the same reference groups, such as the family and peers; nevertheless, the content of the influence varies. Mothers are vital examples of a total life style for both career and non-career-oriented daughters, but career women perceive more persons and a greater diversity of reference groups as affecting their future plans.

Reference Groups

Individuals may hold viewpoints and attitudes quite unlike those of the groups to which they belong. One way to explain this puzzling phenomenon is to recognize that people may orient themselves to other groups, adopting their viewpoints and imitating their behavior. In its brief but busy history, the reference group came to be defined as "any group, collectivity, or person that the actor takes into account in some manner in the course of selecting a behavior from among a set of alternatives, or in making a judgment about a problematic issue" (Kemper, 1968, p. 32). A reference group may or may not be a group to which the individual actually belongs.

Eventually "reference group" came to have several more or less distinguishable meanings. In the first and most general sense, the concept refers to any group whose perspectives constitute a frame of reference for the person. These perspectives can include opinions, beliefs, cognitions, judgments and attitudes—in short, any properties of the reference group that may help the individual to organize her or his perceptions of the environment, including both people and things. A second meaning designates any group serving as a point of reference in making comparisons, especially in forming judgments about one's self (Shibutani, 1955). Individuals may feel rich or poor, capable or incompetent, deprived or endowed, healthy or sick according to the reference group they adopt. Thirdly, the concept can refer to a group to which the individual aspires to belong. Individuals take on the attitudes and behaviors of the reference group in advance of their actual acceptance into it. Because of this anticipatory socialization, the group members may feel that these persons are like themselves in crucial ways and more readily admit them. Hence the process of affiliation is functional for such individuals, since it expedites their social mobility.

There is a danger that the term "reference group" will be used to explain the feelings or perceptions of any persons who differ from the mold of their membership groups. The problem lies in demonstrating that the person is indeed oriented toward some other collectivity. To do this requires ascertaining how and why the individual comes to select some other group as a point of reference. People may select a reference group when relations within their membership group are deteriorating, or when they see a strong possibility of affiliating with the reference group. It is also likely that individuals adopt as reference points those groups which are viewed as socially superior or powerful.

Several groups influence a girl long before she enters school. The family as a reference group obviously is a given, whether the college woman reacts to it positively or negatively. In school, she develops friendships in the natural course of events. And the girl can hardly afford to ignore the presence of college faculty, who are at least powerful, if not otherwise important to students. On a college campus, there are a variety of groups with differing interests, styles, perspectives. Students' past experience may favor receptivity to certain influences rather than others, so the adoption of certain groups in college represents a continuation of previous inclinations, at least to some extent.

Role Models

The significance of a role model is thought to lie in the fact that the neophyte identifies very closely with him or her, consciously or unconsciously attempting to emulate the model. One difficulty with such an approach is that it is hard to understand how the neophyte develops an identity separate from the model, disengaging from a dependent relationship to function competently and independently. Indeed, in extreme cases some individuals appear incapable of doing so. Further, if close identity with and conspicuous copying of the role model occurs, how can the neophyte have sufficient remaining energy to absorb influences from other persons, rather than becoming a carbon copy of the model? An alternative approach incorporating the role-model concept with reference group theory provides a possible solution to these problems.

Kemper (1968) proposes that several types of reference groups are necessary for achievement to occur. *Normative* groups are those which explicitly set norms and espouse values; the individual is expected to comply with these or face negative sanctions for failure. It is highly likely that normative groups are also membership groups, with the family as the chief example. Conformity with the demands of normative groups does not represent achievement but only minimal expected performance. For example, a C grade average is sufficient to allow one to graduate from college, but the student needs an A average to receive honors. In Kemper's view, the individuals go beyond minimal performance when they wish to secure recognition from a second type of reference group, the audience. The *audience* group holds certain values, and people adapt their behavior to accord with those values. The attention of the audience group is sought actively and it, in turn, bestows rewards for performances that meet high standards of excellence. The individual may or may not aspire to become a member of the audience. A college athlete hardly intends to become a member of the crowd that watches him perform; yet he may want to join the ranks of the coaching staff.

Achievement is especially facilitated by one particular type of *comparison* group—the role model:

> Usually an individual rather than a group ... the role model demonstrates for the individual how something is done in the technical sense. [The role model] is concerned with the "how" question. The essential quality of the role model is that he possesses skills and displays techniques which the actor lacks (or things he lacks) and from whom, by observation and comparison with his own performance, the actor can learn. (Kemper, 1968, p. 33)

The pure function of the role model is to provide a technical explication of how a role is to be performed. The role model does not motivate, influence, persuade or reward the actor. In this sense, identification is not a prerequisite for learning from the role model.

Can these analytically distinct types of reference groups be distinguished empirically? Can we determine whether a specific group is serving a normative, an audience or a comparison function? Kemper suggests that the several functions of reference groups may be combined in one group or person and such a fusion of effects may greatly facilitate achievement.

Kemper's scheme becomes even more applicable to the case of college women if we consider career salience and atypicality of occupational choice as special types of achievement. Since prevailing norms direct the female in American society to marry and rear children and to assist the husband's career, the woman who aspires to this life plan is meeting minimal standards. The woman who incorporates career into her plans aspires to more. She does not substitute the career role for the more traditional wife-homemaker one, but chooses an additional set of activities. For most women in the study class the explicit plan and desire to work steadily characterize only the more ambitious ones. Customarily women choose female-dominated occupations, so that the choice of male-dominated work represents a higher level of aspiration, whether the student is conscious of crashing the sex barriers or not.

For women, a variety of reference groups function to shape life-style aspirations, and role models specifically provide demonstrations of how these life styles can be enacted. This is not to assert that the girl clearly perceives who influenced her or in what way. We assume that influences on women's life-style choices operate both explicitly and covertly. The recipient is aware of some influences and not others.

The Family as a Normative Group

When we began this research we assumed that the family would exert a very strong effect on the student's life-style aspirations. Young men favor occupations that are similar to their father's work, and parents urge children to do as well or better than they have. Parents communicate a specific life style. The amount of education they have, the type of work they do and whether the mother works or is active in leisure pursuits should affect the daughter's inclinations. The family is important, as it conveys images of behavior appropriate to a particular social class. Fathers who are professionals or businessmen tend to be strongly committed to their work. In these relatively high-status families, the wife is expected to be a helpmate to her husband and to participate in community and self-enrichment activities. Sometimes clubs, volunteer and charity work become a "career" in themselves. Daughters in such families are less likely to aspire to a career than are daughters from families where "male" and "provider" are not so inextricably linked.

The list of family variables influencing children's aspirations could become very long, especially for male offspring.

As a first and primary reference group, the potential of the family is indeed strong. With this in mind, we examined as many family variables as we could to find their connection with career planning. With the exception of maternal employment, however, we found little relation between career salience and parental characteristics.

The fathers of non-career aspirers do have somewhat higher level occupations—they are slightly more likely to be executives, managers, proprietors or officials than are the fathers of career-salient women. The two groups do not differ in terms of father's income, education, or overall social class position, although the fathers of career women are a bit more likely to be self-employed. The mothers of career and non-career students are similar in age, amount of education, and in occupational training. The women are equally likely to have a large city as their hometown.

The data on family structure are a little puzzling. Career-oriented women less often have sisters and less often have brothers than the non-career-oriented women, yet they are no more likely to be a firstborn or only child. Neither group has a high number of divorced or deceased parents. Hence the presence or absence of family members bears little relation to career plans.

One other among the 17 family variables we considered is connected with career salience—religion. While the study class is roughly equally divided among Protestants, Catholics and Jews, Catholic girls are unlikely to be career oriented or to choose a male-dominated occupation and Jewish girls are especially likely to plan for a career in a male-dominated field. Protestant students fall in between these two extremes. This finding accords well with other research regarding religiosity (Lenski, 1961). Catholic groups are usually found to be somewhat conservative on social issues, and Catholic students have been less likely to develop high educational aspirations than other groups. By contrast, Jewish families promote very high educational and occupational aspirations among their children (Feldman and Newcomb, 1969).

The Mother as a Role Model

The special influence that family exerts seems to come mainly via the mother as a role model for her daughter. We could find no unique influence by the father. Rather, the same-sex parent seems to be the most influential for girls.

We compiled detailed work histories of the students' mothers from questionnaire data. Fully half of the non-career-oriented students report that their mothers have never worked; this is true for only one fifth of the career aspirers (Table 8-1). Over half the mothers of career-oriented girls worked while the students were in school, providing for them a vivid demonstration of how to combine family and work. Perhaps girls with working mothers learn a more favorable definition of the working-mother role, especially since their fathers do not object strenuously. In only one instance did a girl report that she had been unhappy and frustrated because her mother worked. Her father was dead and she resented being shunted from one housekeeper to another.

Apparently holding a job does not detract appreciably from the mothers' involvement in leisure activities. Career and non-career students are highly likely to have a mother who is active in some sort of extra-familial pursuit. The mothers of the career aspirers are slightly more selective in their activities; they are typically involved in only one while the mothers of non-career-oriented students often have two or more activities involving clubs or organizations, community or volunteer work. The career-oriented women report that their mothers have hobbies or participate in sports. These are more likely individual or solo activities, while the other mothers participate more heavily in organized groups.

Table 8-1. Mother's Work and Leisure Activities

	Non-career oriented	Career oriented	Q value
Mother never worked	52%	22%	.59*
Mother worked during student's college years	26%	56%	.57**
Mother has leisure activities	70%	70%	.00

* Chi square = 8.27, with 1 df, at p = .01
** Chi square = 8.10, with 1 df, at p = .01
+ For an explanation of Yale's Q, a measure of association, see Appendix 2: Life Style Index, and Davis (1971).

Most daughters accept the definition of the feminine role portrayed by their mothers. Consider the contrast between the following two students:

I have always been proud of my mother. My father does not have a college education, but my mother does. She went to school ten years at night and got a diploma when she was pregnant with my younger brother. Since I was about eight or nine she has worked as an accountant part time with a very flexible schedule. She likes communicating with people. She has always been sociable and agressive, whereas I have just developed this in the last two or three years. So my mother has been a great influence. I always looked at my mother and saw she worked and I said I am going to college and I am going to have a career, too.

My mother has never really worked since we were born, although she worked before she married. I would want to work for a year or two after I got married until there are children. It might help me to understand any problems that my husband would come home with. I would want to work just to get some experience and to use my education. But my mother didn't work and I don't want to either.

Another student whose mother had gone back to work during the student's college years felt this had encouraged her own plans to pursue a career:

My mother is working part time now, she teaches two days a week and there are two little ones at home, aged seven and ten. She is so much happier. She is a changed woman. She went to graduate school this summer, adding a semester toward her master's degree. . . . All of a sudden she realized that she really was [smart]. I mean my father is very smart, But sometimes she felt that dad was always the smart one. But she is doing very well. She got two A's and she was excited to be learning about things. She understood the things I have been telling her about the poverty programs and the difficulty of teaching [culturally deprived] children. She now does more things with my brother and sister. They have a happier home life. She is doing things now that before she would not have had time to do. She is going out twice a week and having to look nice. I come home and she looks younger than she did before.

The home-oriented mother also constitutes a model for her daughter:

Our family life has been kind of strange. My father even has a little bell he rings and my mother comes running and brings him coffee and he will call her from another room to change the television station. And it has been so successful. He is so happy and she is happy doing it. Why not treat him like a king because the male ego is kind of a sensitive thing to go tampering with. My life is probably not going to make that much difference on society, but maybe what my husband and children do will. I don't feel that I am that important, but if I had the time left over, I would like to do volunteer work or spend time on my own hobbies. *If* I have the time left over.

The students' words are reminiscent of other research (Baruch 1972a) that finds that college women "whose mothers have not worked devalue feminine competence. Career-related achievement is apparently defined as masculine by women who have not been exposed to a maternal model of work competence." In another report, Baruch (1972b) reveals that the daughter's identification with her mother is significantly stronger if the mother works, and that this identification is positive so that the daughter admires her mother's ability to have both a career and a family.

Collegiate Reference Groups

Once in college, there are departmental organizations, special interest societies, honoraries, sororities, both male and female friends, peers in the same major, faculty and department—these are the major groups with which students may affiliate. Let us begin with the more formally organized extracurricular activities. The two activities students mention most are the Greek organizations and the departmental clubs, such as the chemical society, home economics club and student publications. Two thirds of the class describe themselves as moderately or very active in extracurricular groups, and career and non-career aspirers do not differ appreciably in their overall level of involvement (Table 8-2). But career aspirers are significantly less frequently sorority members. Twenty-nine percent of careerists belong, compared with 76 percent of non-careerists.

The difference in sorority membership is striking, and reveals that non-career women affiliate with quite different groups than the career oriented, who are more involved in departmental clubs. These professionally centered organizations tie the student to her major, give her experience within a discipline, and allow her to explore career opportunities. On the other hand, sorority is devoted largely to fulfilling sociability functions. The Greeks organize most of the campus-wide social events and provide clear dating opportunities:

> The sorority helped me to get acquainted with a lot of people. Well, I got to know a lot of the fellows in my pin-mate's fraternity and when we broke up I started dating them. The sorority lets you know which fraternities are the good ones and which ones to avoid.

When we asked students what had been the most satisfying thing to them each year, one common reply was:

The most satisfying thing is working in my sorority. The sorority gives you the group, the closely knit group with whom you can work, and it organizes things that you could not otherwise achieve on campus or just by yourself. It is a very fulfilling experience.

Table 8-2. College Activities

	Non-career oriented	Career oriented	Q value
Belongs to sorority	76%	39%	–.66*
Extracurricular activities (moderately or very active)	67%	71%	.07
Dating frequency in college (once a week or more)	70%	78%	.21
Marital status, senior year (single, not going steady)	46%	61%	.30

* Chi square = 12.27, with 1 df, p = .01.

Whether sororities are closely knit or amorphous, integral or an appendage to campus life, our findings about them concur with Scott's (1965) appraisal that the sorority functions largely as a parental surrogate in maintaining social class and ethnic endogamy. Its activities are diverse but oriented primarily toward forming alliances with appropriate males from socially equal fraternities. Sororities invite fraternities and are invited by them in turn to mixers and dances. They hold parties when members become pinned, and engagements are celebrated enthusiastically. Pledge classes are drilled in proper manners. Older students teach the new member how to dress and talk with members of the opposite sex. In these ways the sorority combines the several functions of reference groups. It provides normative sanctions for finding a marriage partner, role models to facilitate the learning of behavior to attract males, and rewards for individuals successful in their quest. The sorority provides a unique framework for encouraging marriage.

Relationships with Male Peers

Despite the sorority findings, we found no significant differences between career and non-career aspirers in frequency of dating (Table 8-2). In addition to dating patterns, we carefully reviewed the data to determine whether some connection exists between a girl's relationship with a male and her career plans. As Table 8-2 shows, there is only a slight tendency (not statistically significant) for non-career women to be attached to a male—career women tend to be unattached, single or not going steady. Bayer (1972) notes that women who rate themselves high academically and students of both sexes at selective schools are less prone to marry during college. He finds that students of both sexes are apparently good predictors of the likelihood that they will marry, and that women with higher degree aspirations tend not to marry as undergraduates.

Student comments suggest that career plans and conceptions about family are formed before the alliance with a specific marriage partner occurs. One girl explained that her career plans motivated her to discontinue dating a boy whose views differ from hers:

> When I first came to school I had a boyfriend whose attitude was very much that the husband should work and provide the money and the woman should stay at home and cook and have children. That is one reason why we broke up, because I did not agree with him.

Even girls with atypical career plans can balance them with plans to be married, particularly if their fiancé is willing. One girl who will be marrying soon is applying to the same graduate school as her boyfriend. When asked if she thought that getting married would affect her plans for the future, she replied:

> No. I probably wouldn't have kept going out with him if he didn't see things the way I did. A lot of people don't like women to work after they are married at all. . . . He doesn't mind. He is the one who pushed me to go to graduate school. I always wanted to just work before, but he said to me, "Start looking because you like school and you enjoy your courses. So if you want to, why not?" So I started looking [for graduate schools to attend].

Future husbands seem to give shape to explicit plans without altering basic career or non-career expectations. One student says her boy friend expresses his ideas about what occupation she should choose:

> He wants me to go into designing. We talk about it a lot and he is really excited about it. He also feels that if I want to go into social work, that is OK too. . . . He just doesn't want me to teach.

In these respects the future male functions somewhat as an audience for the girl. For example, a non-career-oriented student finds a marriage partner whom she perceives as agreeing with her plans:

> I would like to work for a few years to get into something that I could probably come back to later on. It also depends on many factors. The fellow I am going to marry is not opposed to my working. If we have children it will be once they are in high school before I work, and he might try to keep it to something part-time, but he is fairly open-minded about the fact that women need something besides their home and family to keep them occupied, especially if they have gone to college.

The students, then, reveal some interdependence between career plans and relationship with a particular male. Some women stop dating a male because he does not agree with their plans; some rather actively seek a male who does agree; and others, a rare few, have boyfriends who encourage their motivation for a career. Very few women report that a male friend influenced their occupational choice directly. Most who were both career oriented and planning marriage could make their plans for graduate school or work fit with their fiancé's plans. Virtually none indicated a cessation of interest in career as a result of becoming attached to a male.

One specific factor distinguishes the careerists from the non-career aspirers. Career women are the only group to mention discussing career plans with males to whom they are not attached romantically. A student who had selected law was asked if she felt any particular persons influenced her choice:

> I got interested while I was down in Washington, D.C., the last two summers. I worked for a lawyer in the department of Housing and Urban Development. I did a lot of work there that was pertinent [to law] and I also had a lot of friends working in law firms and they all started to pressure me, you know, why don't you go to law school. . . .

From the questionnaire we could judge the degree of similarity between occupations chosen by the students and their friends. We considered occupations similar if they were alike either in subject matter or profession. Examples of similar fields are computer work and mathematics; similar professions are English teacher and history teacher. Most of the students choose occupations similar to those reportedly chosen by female friends, but career-salient women more often make choices similar to those of male friends. This may be partly due to the likelihood that career-salient women choose male-dominated occupations, or that they perceive persons of both sexes as influential in their occupational choice. But it especially suggests that career women interact concerning occupational pursuits with persons from both sexes rather than females alone. Sharing ideas about one's professional future with males is qualitatively different from planning a home and children with a boyfriend. The career girl has male friends interested in occupations similar to her preference, and the contact with males helps clarify her own career goals.

Teachers and Occupational Role Models

Women who are career oriented and choose a male-dominated occupation are most often influenced by role models, either professors or persons in an occupation, while the non-career women perceive family members or no one as exerting a special effect on their plans. Families direct their daughters largely toward occupations that can be worked at "just in case," those that the person can leave and re-enter easily. Frequently students have relatives who are teachers. Sometimes they sense an impetus to play out the social-service values their parents hold. In short, the family stimulates students toward enterprising or pioneering fields mainly when the mother herself is employed; otherwise the family moves the girl away from career interests.

Teachers exert a clearer influence. The selection of faculty members as significant reference persons is crucial for moving women toward careers. For our study participants, faculty are more potent for the career aspirers. It is not the whole faculty within a department that affects the students. Instead, one or two professors hold the attention of career aspirers. This is probably a two-way street; both professor and student contribute to the relationship. The professor displays the skills and life style associated with a particular occupational role or a related one, and, in a sense, invites the student to consider choosing it for herself. In these respects the professor serves most auspiciously as a role model.

A prime function of role models is to enable the novice to grasp first-hand knowledge about particular occupational roles. Students learn the tasks required, something about the context in which the work is carried out, and glimpse the hierarchy of positions through which practitioners advance.

In the university there are daily opportunities to observe professors as teachers and researchers. Students can infer the values associated with the academic world and may come to know something about the extra-work pursuits of the faculty. If they catch on to these salient life-style aspects and admire them, professors may serve just as other work-role models do.

A subtle influence process operates between career-oriented women and their professors. When we asked women how the faculty view them as students, 81 percent of career aspirers said that their teachers consider them outstanding or bright. This is significantly higher than the 60 percent of non-career women who thought their teachers consider them bright. Thus, the career women incorporate a self-image as able, competent and bright—reflecting the positive opinions of their chief evaluators during college. Perhaps the faculty do merely what comes naturally: teach, explain, expound and proselytize for their own disciplines. In so doing, professors reward those students who perform ably and express interest. The student is flattered by professional attention, the mentor is pleased to find recruits.

Since all the students as seniors achieve rather good grades (B average or higher), it is clear that high grades alone do not explain career interests. But among career-oriented women, a small number become "converts" to career during their sophomore and junior years. At that stage, their grades rose sharply. So for this subgroup of careerists, especially, the conversion process seems to involve first getting noticeably better grades and then coming around to career aspirations. The converts seem to be reminded, via their academic performance, that they *are* bright and therefore ought to pursue careers. This is a kind of mirroring effect, involving the student's performance, the teacher's view of that performance, and the student's view of the teacher's view (Cf. Thielens, 1971)!

This sort of influence can lead students to raise their aspirations. Some women undergo a mild conversion experience when they begin to think of themselves in a new light. They express delight and surprise:

> It never really seemed like a practical thing to do, to major in history. But I got hung up on one particular course taught by a professor here, and he was very encouraging. For some reason he was satisfied with most of what I was doing. I guess I always sort of figured, well you are in history and some day you will teach. As soon as it occurred to me that I might possibly be fellowship material, I immediately assumed that I could go into college teaching.

So the professor may think quite highly of the student's ability, and let her know of his appraisal. But the teacher need not heap unrelenting praise on the student; he or she is careful to point out areas for improvement:

> Recently I have been talking to Professor G. She is the first person I showed my work to, and because of the praise that she showered on me and the criticism that she gave me, I felt confident in going on. She seems to think I can write.

Such a relationship is likely to occur when students work closely with a teacher either in independent study courses or as an employee. The salience of the professor as role model should be evident from the fact that one fourth of the class chose college teaching or advanced research work as their preferred career. More than any other group these students were involved directly and continuously with one or more faculty members in an apprenticeship role.

Much specific role-model influence occurs outside the university, within an explicit work situation. Career-oriented women have many more experiences of this kind. Two thirds of them have held two or more different jobs, compared with less than one third of the non-career aspirers. Other work-role models are simply friends, sometimes previous graduates of the university, and sometimes they are married women, so that students see a woman implementing a dual role:

> I've only got three more semesters, but after I graduate I can still get the credits required for a teacher's certificate. I know an art teacher in Maryland whose job lets her go to the students that have to stay home. She visits them two or three times a week. When her own children are at school she's working, and yet it still gives her time to take care of the house and be with her family at lunch time when they come home.

Another student tells how she obtained her image of the field of merchandising:

> I know a girl who graduated from here last year. I have met some people just by working downtown and I have other contacts like that. My boyfriend's aunt is in merchandising, so I think I have a realistic picture of what it is all about.

We cannot judge from our study exactly what effect the sex of the work-role model has on career interests. Students describe some men and some women in glowing terms and others in deprecating ways. Women students are likely to have male role models within the university, if only because the faculty is predominantly male. We considered it likely that career-oriented women students would come from fields with high proportions of women faculty. Yet career-women students were most common in the social sciences and humanities, fields with about one-fourth women on their faculties. And career-oriented students least often stemmed from the home economics fields, which had close to 100 percent female faculty. Nevertheless, throughout the university, women comprised only about 10 percent of the total faculty so that students may "observe the rarity of the phenomenon and infer the conditions which keep it so" (Gold, 1968). Furthermore, the students suggested that, despite their own professional roles, the home economics faculty valued domesticity, the homemaking arts and traditional sex roles. By contrast, both men and women faculty in the male-dominated and mixed sex fields encouraged more pioneering career choices in the women students. The few women faculty in these fields may provide the specific comparison group against which college girls can match themselves. A woman English professor and famous novelist —a renowned teacher who was married and reared a family and published numerous books—was the idol revered by many of the students and much referred to in the interviews.

Who Influences Career Women?

As the college years proceed, women remain affected by their mother's example. Mothers who stay home to raise the family usually have daughters who want to do just that. Mothers who work seem to show their daughters the feasibility of combining a job with domesticity—they may also be communicating their personal rewards from work. We do not know how the working mothers see themselves, as career women or not. Nevertheless, the mother's actual role influences her daughter's aspirations.

In the realm of college life, sorority encourages women to pursue traditional aims, to find a mate and have a family. But male friends and classmates foster career interests. We cannot claim that these influences are casual. More likely there is a reciprocity between the girl's initial inclinations and her choice of peers: if she is traditional, she's more prone to join sorority anyway; if she's less conventional, both peers and professors become important reference groups for her. The interaction between professors and career aspirers is particularly subtle; professors notice bright students and encourage them; in turn, these students seek contact with faculty.

It looks as if women who develop career interests are exposed to a broad range of people and experiences both before and during college, a broader world of options than their more conventional classmates. Beginning with her own family, the careerist seeks and finds co-workers, peers and professors whose lives and interests she admires, whose roles she tries to emulate. They, in turn, recognize her abilities and encourage her to use them.

*Throughout this chapter, and in the remainder of the book, we use the terms career-oriented or career-salient or career aspirer to refer to the measure described as the Life Style Index. The Index is a composite measure: high scorers are career salient while low scorers are non-career salient. High career salience refers to women who plan postgraduate training, seek work providing freedom from supervision, want to work even if their husbands earn enough and even when their children are young, and who see themselves as future career women. Low or non-career oriented women plan no further education, are unlikely to work if their husbands' earnings are adequate, do not want to work while their children are young and see themselves as future housewives.

9   Career Women Are Different, Not Deviant

What does it take to become an outstanding scientist? Scientists of note are characterized by high intellectual ability, an intense chanelling of energy in one direction, extreme independence and apartness from others (Roe, 1963; Rossi, 1965). Since girls are reared to stress the opposite of these characteristics, how are they to become scientists? In fact, pursuit of a professional career takes some of these same ingredients. Yet women have been more people-oriented and concerned with helping others. They may fear being considered unfeminine if they enter engineering and the sciences, fields peopled mainly by men. Or women may avoid the sciences and medicine because they consider these fields too demanding for a woman who wants to combine work with family responsibilities and who prefer work that is part-time (Rossi, 1965).

All of this might lead to the conclusion that no women ever try to become scientists, engineers or physicians or to pursue any other professional fields. Not at all. Small numbers have done so for a long time. And the proportion of women entering some fields has been inching up. Between 1969 and 1970, women accounted for substantially greater enrollment increases than men in engineering, the physical sciences, medicine and law (DHEW, 1971). Despite the still minuscule representations of women in these fields, some mysterious conditions must bring them where few women have tread and where the terrain is known to be rough.

As work increasingly becomes a normal part of women's lives, the seesaw tips, so that women who enter home could become the "deviants." If it is common for women to enter (or re-enter) the labor force once their children are grown, then the woman who does not becomes suspect. Indeed, a follow-up study of women in their early fifties who had been hospitalized for psychiatric illness ten years earlier showed them as more "home-bound" than the control group of their neighbors who had never been treated for mental disorder (Molholm and Dinitz, 1972). Compared with the normal women, the ex-patients concentrated on homemaking and family, largely avoiding work and social activities outside the home. Home served as a "sheltered workshop," insulating the ex-patients from the stresses of the outside world (Angrist, Dinitz, Molholm, 1972). Social scientists have only begun to unravel the interconnections between sex roles and psychiatric illness (Gove and Tudor, 1973). However, we do know that there will always be perfectly healthy, normal, competent women who truly do not prefer to work, who enjoy the housewife, mother and volunteer roles. It is our fervent hope that such options continue to be available without stigma or personal cost to women.

At the other extreme remain the women, still considered deviants, who choose not merely to work. They want to make work their focal life interest, as many men do. They opt for careers against great odds. The career woman, like working women in general, has to keep asking herself: Why not? Why can't I be a doctor, lawyer, scientist, writer, architect? As she takes stock of her life potential, she chooses the variety, novelty, commitment, challenge and hard work that a career offers. "And in the array of book, crib, men, laboratory, and office, these women have said: Put them together, it takes more doing, but with that variety, it cannot be dull" (Luria, 1972, p. 33).

Early in her life, the career-bound woman, must encounter some approval for her abilities, interests and individuality. Perhaps she is rewarded in her motivation to succeed, perhaps she excels her classmates in academic performance and is recognized as intellectually able, perhaps she works hard and is encouraged to do so (Frieze, 1974). In the last chapter we began to explain the contrast between women who end college as career aspirers and those who do not. We showed how people and situations influence a girl's aspirations: her mother's life style, teachers, peers and work contacts seem potent factors in the girl's own preferences.

It is the career-oriented girls whose mothers tend to work and participate little in community work, clubs and other leisure pursuits. It is mothers of the non-career oriented who actively pursue leisure involvements but do not hold jobs. In one case, the mother shows how to combine marriage and work satisfactorily; in the other case, she indicates that family and leisure activities go together, but work does not.

Apart from her mother, the girl is exposed to other adults, men and women, who either serve as role models or else encourage or discourage her own inclinations. Particularly positive rewards come from relationships with people, especially professors, who exhibit work skills and meet work demands and whose enjoyment of work may move a woman toward career.

Even college peers and friends play a part: sorority, by its conventional conceptions about sex roles, attracts the non-career woman, but its value may push the early career aspirer away from such ambitions. And male compatriots radiate their own occupational concerns, which can affect female acquaintances. Thus career-oriented women are more interested in male-dominated occupations and share some male views about the kind of work they find desirable.

This cumulative picture of the study participants is striking because of the unusual features of the career-oriented women. Their backgrounds and experiences appear to offer a different *weltanschauung* from the traditional sex-role orientations. Perhaps this is mere differentness. Or could it be strong deviation from the normative developmental pattern? The career aspiring women seem to be products of additional, insight-provoking experiences, a growing-up process that leads them to hold a less stereotyped and broader conception of appropriate female roles. Unlike radical feminists, they may not totally reject the customary, time-honored duties of women so much as augment these aspects by work as an essential feature of adult life. They seem to have positive inducements for aspiring to a career, including the direct impact of role models and the indirect influence of important reference groups. This we call an "enrichment view" of career aspirers.

Career Interests as Deviant

Other researchers have either stressed or implied that women who aspire to a career are deviants, socially and psychologically. They are depicted as rare individuals whose plans to pursue work regularly and continuously are unconventional, especially those who select male-dominated occupations. This image comes from the pens of researchers whose explanations differ slightly—some describe conflicted female relationships or faulty sex-role learning, others talk of social rejection and isolation as causes for turning toward career.

In these terms, the conventional woman, who may work but is mainly home oriented, accepts a complex but relatively well-defined set of normative expectations for her adult roles. The career-oriented woman is viewed as the product of social learning experiences that set her apart from more conventional age-mates, experiences leading to a masculine self-image.

Women with their traits and sex-role experiences learn very early to be "feminine" or likeable, to get along with people, to be nurturant, passive, and expressive emotionally, to favor affiliation rather than achievement (Hoffman, 1972). These are not considered qualities that make for persistence and concentration on a career. Therefore, women who are interested in careers and in choosing male-dominated fields can certainly be defined as deviant in terms both of personal characteristics *and* occupational choice. More than that, the very notion of women as career oriented suggests deviance from the current normative conception of work as a peripheral, limited feature of a woman's adult life.

The research literature favors such a view of career women as deviant, unconventional, even maladjusted. A classic statement, based on scanty evidence, is this portrayal of "The Career Girl":

> In a sense, girls who plan for a career are less well adjusted than those who are content to become housewives. Not only is the career-oriented girl likely to have a rather poor self-concept, but she also probably lacks a close relationship with her family. (Lewis, 1968, p. 33)

Lewis stresses the career girl's turning away from the family for role models and claims that her future role differs radically from her mother's traditional example. Hence he infers that a woman's career orientation may lead to frustration and dissatisfaction, or that she seeks career as sublimation for her personal dissatisfaction. Either way "the road to good adjustment, for women, is that which stays within the traditional feminine role ..." (Lewis, 1968, p. 34).

Even studies of college men incorporate the idea that breaking out of conventional status boundaries such as socioeconomic level is related to a conflicted family situation. Upward mobility striving and high achievement orientations presumably derive from troubles in the family. Dynes and associates (1956) found that students with high mobility aspirations differ from low aspirers in that they had experienced feelings of rejection more frequently. Moreover, they think their parents show more favoritism toward a brother or sister, they feel less emotional attachment to parents, and point to a lesser degree of happiness during childhood.

A similar hypothesis is that individuals who experience a depriving family of orientation are more likely to have mobility aspirations than those from a satisfying milieu. The respondents were asked whether their family situation was happy or unhappy, and to compare their situation to that of other teen-agers. They were also queried about relationships with each parent. The association between deprivation and aspiration was supported only by the father-daughter relationship. Rushing (1964) concludes that there is a connection between father-daughter relationships, sex-role identity and adoption of the career role:

> When the father-daughter relationship is depriving, the daughter may generalize this unpleasant relationship to males in general. She may shun intimate relationships with all males, thus rejecting the role of wife and mother. In addition she may strive for higher status as a means to compensate for the lack of reward derived from her father . . . as well as the foregone rewards associated with the status of wife and mother. (Rushing, 1964, p. 166.)

A corollary hypothesis is advanced by Miriam Johnson (1963). According to her, boys and girls both initially identify with the mother, but their relationship is not sex-typed. Identification with the father, especially after the infantile dependence stage, is crucial for proper sex role learning to occur. The male role actually has two components, with the father acting instrumentally toward the son and expressively toward the daughter. If the father-daughter relationship is not a solidary one, she does not develop the expressive feminine role. Thus, a girl needs not just a mother to emulate, she also needs a father with whom she can practice her femininity. She plays woman to the man.

There is other evidence for this hypothesis that emotional deprivation leads to aspiration. For example, Ellis (1952) found differences between socially mobile and non-mobile unmarried women. All were outstanding in terms of their jobs and professions; they were judged mobile or non-mobile in relation to their father's occupation. Larger proportions of the mobile women experienced rejection by their general community and at least partial rejection by their parents. During adulthood, these women were more isolated socially, had fewer intimate friends, briefer friendships and more conflict with parents during adulthood.

These findings—that women's career orientation and high mobility aspirations are linked to unsatisfactory family situations—are quite puzzling. They are especially puzzling because there is strong evidence from other studies that career aspirers have special socialization experiences but not necessarily negative ones.

Career Aspirations as Enrichment

Alice Rossi (1967) proposes that women career aspirants differ from the modal pattern of development and interests characteristic of their contemporaries. In other words, women who end up in careers learned to be different in their growing up. This proposition finds support in research on women graduates from 135 colleges: highly career-oriented women were less likely to be married or to have children if married; to show low valuation of family roles; to have begun dating later; to have dated less in high school and college; to enjoy less young children, visiting, relatives, planning and organizing; and to have been consistently higher in reading, study, and solo activities than non-career-salient women.

These results can be interpreted in different ways. One can say that women who pursue careers are pushed out of the family and consequently out of the feminine mold, they are forced into careers rather than choosing, they are socially isolated and rejected instead of being people who prefer solitary pursuits.

The alternative interpretation says that career women are different rather than deviant, they recognize the wider

options offered by family, friends, teachers and acquaintances, their growing up was freer, more open to alternatives,
more conducive to independence and achievement. Such a
view also receives support in the literature, but it lacks clear
labeling.

In one study, eight-and eleven-year-old children were asked
whether behaviors such as driving a car, washing dishes, or
working in an office belonged to men, to women, or to both.
The children's responses paralleled those of adults. Girls
whose mothers were in the labor force sex-typed fewer items
(63 percent) than girls whose mothers were not working (81
percent). The mother's work status was more decisive than
the children's age or sex, with the children of working
mothers showing greater variation in response and a more
egalitarian view of role activities (Hartley, 1960).

Among a very small sample of college women, the only
family variable significantly related to the student's desire to
work in the future was the mother's own work history (Siegal
and Curtis, 1963). Kinnard White (1967) found that among
in-service teachers, one factor related to commitment to
teaching as a career was their mothers' work history.

The expectations of significant adults, like the husband,
are tied to the woman's life style. Men whose wives work
differ from men whose wives are not employed (Axelson,
1963). They are more likely to agree that wives should work
even if there is no financial emergency, and they tend to
think that personal choice is the main reason for wives to
work. As compared to the husbands of non-working wives
they less often agree that children should be through school
before the wife assumes a job. They more often agree that
they should help around the house whether or not the wife is
employed. All this suggests that husbands of working wives
hold a more liberal view of sex roles and an egalitarian
conception of family life. Husbands of non-working wives are
likely to think working would be detrimental to the children
and that a wife would become too independent if she held a
job and would be less of a companion than if she did not

work. They think they would feel inadequate in the provider role if a wife earned more than they did. They perceive an employed wife as a threat to their masculine prerogatives and the well-being of their children.

It is not clear whether a man's attitudes are more favorable because the wife is working or whether the favorable attitudes initially led the woman to seek work. Both factors are probably mutually reinforcing, although we are cautious in interpreting these findings because there was also poorer marital adjustment among families in which the wife worked full time rather than in families where the wife worked part-time or not at all (Axelson, 1963). Orden and Bradburn (1969) point out that among couples where the wife can freely choose whether to work, there is a higher net balance of marital satisfactions over tensions than in families where she feels it necessary to work.

Testing the Deviance Hypothesis

The social component of the deviance hypothesis implies that career women are social rejects, uninvolved with peers and with dating. This is not borne out in our study. As we reported earlier, career-salient women do not date less in college, nor are they less active in campus affairs than their more conventional classmates. But they do stand out in their lesser involvement with sororities, and the careerists are less often going steady, engaged or married.

Perceptions of Parents

But one may protest that, after all, relationships with peers are less crucial for personal development than relationships with parents. So we checked this aspect of the deviance hypothesis that women who aspire to careers grow up in unhappy, strained or conflicted relationships with their parents. This view assumes that women pursue careers because their parents reject them or fail to offer a close, warm relationship. The daughter is omitted from the intimate family circle; family and motherhood become negative points of reference. Psychiatric interviews would probably be necessary to test these assumptions fully. Our approach was to ask respondents to check from a list of eight statements all those which describe their mother, their father, or both parents. The negative items were:

Dismisses my problems as unimportant.

Hard to talk to.

Often criticizes me unfairly.

Has little free time.

The positive items were:

Gives me advice.

Offers sympathy and affection.

Helps me with my problems.

Is a good listener.

As freshmen, all the women had a slightly more positive image of their parents than they held as seniors (Table 9-1). In that year, non-career-oriented women were only slightly more likely to attribute positive characteristics to their parents (76 percent compared with 66 percent) and somewhat more career-oriented women attributed negative characteristics to their parents (38 versus 28 percent). But the relationships between life-style aspirations and perception of parental qualities is very weak and statistically nonsignificant. The trend does not emphasize any difference between the two groups in terms of the mother alone, father alone or both parents together. The absolute difference in the number of positive or negative items checked is negligible. Thus differences in career plans cannot be traced to poor relationships with parents that exist during college. However, the tendency for careerists to view their parents more critically may suggest that as these women pass through the four years of college and begin to formulate career plans they also grow

**Table 9-1. Parental Relationships, Maladjustment and
Life Style Aspirations of Seniors**

	Career oriented	Non-career oriented	Q value
Attributes positive features to parents	66%	76%	–.26
Attributes negative features to parents	38	28	.12
College maladjustment (high score)	51	41	.19

away from their parents. That movement could increase with
time. Still, we are loathe to see this as conflict—it could also
represent growing independence and self-sufficiency as Gump
(1972) suggests.

College Maladjustment

We should explore beyond the family to see if career interests
arise out of personal maladjustment or problems that develop
during college. Perhaps women seek careers because they
can't "cut it" socially on campus, or they don't like
university life except academically. Or conversely, an interest
in career could alienate a girl from her less achievement-
oriented friends and classmates; hence she may become
maladjusted because of her special interests.

We measured maladjustment with the College Maladjustment Scale (Kleinmuntz, 1960 and 1961). The Mt Scale is a
43-item test drawn from the larger Minnesota Multiphasic
Personality Inventory. The test successfully distinguishes
maladjusted from adjusted college students in terms of
manifestation of specific behaviors, fears and problems. We
could find no association either for freshmen or seniors
between life-style aspirations and maladjustment: the product moment correlations were low and negative both for

freshmen (r = -.18) and seniors (r = -.004). Again, there is a slight hint that the career oriented score higher on maladjustment but there is no strong or statistically significant relationship.

In order to assess the validity of this lack of difference in Mt scores, we used a "harder" behavioral measure on which to compare the career and non-career women. The two groups were compared on their use of the university counseling center during the four years. We defined counselees as women who had one or more visits. We found that 36 percent of career-oriented women were counseled compared with 15 percent of non-career aspirers.

While overall few women received counseling, we must unravel this seeming discrepancy between the absence of maladjustment difference and the presence of counseling differences. First, we may recall that the Mt scale is an indirect measure of personality maladjustment. But seeking counseling is a direct reflection of need for help, information or guidance. Thus, having sought counseling may mean a girl perceives herself as maladjusted or having problems despite the fact that an objective test shows her not to be more problematic than is normal. Her own perception does not jibe with the objective evaluation. Or, second, seeking counseling may reflect a girl's desire to understand herself, or to obtain vocational guidance or help with a dating problem. It need not define the seeker-for-help as maladjusted. Career-oriented girls may thus be the very ones who want to explore their potential and their options in life, both at college and later. Thus, they seek guidance for self-enrichment purposes rather than to cope with their deviance. Still another interpretation would hold that the college period is too early for assessing maladjustment as a function of career interest, that only when a woman actually pursues a career as a central life involvement does her deviant personality develop strongly.

Lacking further evidence, we cannot quarrel with any of the three arguments. We propose a view of career women as curious and searching, seeking help to formulate goals, perhaps even to cope with pressures to stay traditional. Our positive picture of career aspirers gets more support from a look at their sex-role conceptions.

Sex-Role Conceptions

The deviance hypothesis explicitly contains the notion that women with career interests differ appreciably from normative views of appropriate behavior for men and women. Career aspirers are supposed to reject marriage and motherhood. Such a view is patently false, at least for the students in our study, since 96 percent of them expect to marry and eventually rear children. The career oriented do disagree with the non-career oriented in how they envision handling family and domestic responsibilities and in their conceptions of the maternal role.

First, while the career-oriented women are just as interested in getting married as the non-careerists, they are more willing to postpone marriage. About half say twenty-four or older is an ideal age to be married. Only a fourth of the family oriented are willing to defer the wedding bells so long. Second, the two groups of women are in sharp disagreement over how to rear children. Well over half of the non-career oriented, but only one fifth of the career-salient students, feel very strongly that it is important for a mother to care personally for her children throughout the day (Table 9-2).

Non-career women were vocal in the interviews on the importance of their presence at home during the years when their children are young. It is unfortunate that the reader cannot hear the vehement voice of the student who said:

> I will be teaching until the family starts, but I don't intend to teach again until they are grown. I don't believe in parents leaving their children with housemothers or whatever they are. I want to raise my own.

Table 9-2. Sex-Role Conceptions and Life Style Aspirations of Seniors

	Career oriented	Non-career oriented	Q value
Values personal child-care very strongly	20%	57%	−.68*
Desires marriage at age (24 or older)	44	24	.42**
Sex-role ideology score traditional	20	59	−.70***

  * Chi square = 12.47 with 1 df, p = .001
 ** Chi square = 3.89 with 1 df, p = .05
*** Chi square = 13.84 with 1 df, p = .001

Career women raised the issue less frequently. Only one student expressed the possibility that children might not fit her plans at all. She was asked whether she planned to continue working after marriage. Her reply:

> I would never consider stopping. Well at this point we are not considering having children within the next ten years. I sort of think that is a crime to our society and to yourself to slave for all these years and become a productive scientist and then say, "I'll see you in 15 years after my children are grown up." You are 15 years behind. You might as well not start at the rate science is going. If I want children they are just going to have to be worked in.

It is interesting to note that this young woman was then already engaged to be married and that her fiancé concurred with her viewpoint.

Other career women are highly ambivalent about leaving child-care to others, so they compromise either by planning part-time work or by delaying career pursuits until their children enter school.

Students responded to a set of five items concerning their ideas of the appropriate household division of labor (Hoffman, 1963). In the first year of college, both groups express fairly traditional sex-role ideology. Only those who become career-oriented discard this perspective, and the difference in ideology between the two groups widens dramatically. By senior year the careerists are significantly less likely to believe that "raising children is more a mother's job than a father's." They more often disagree with the statement that "the wife should do the cooking and housecleaning and the husband should provide the family with money." The non-career women more readily profess the virtues of separate roles for men and women. They more often agree that "if the man is working to support the family, his wife has no right to expect him to work when he's home," that "a man who helps around the kitchen is doing more than should be expected," and that a man ought to feel free to relax when he gets home from work."

Students sometimes support their non-career orientation with the premise that domestic responsibilities prohibit work commitment:

> I would never let a family eat TV dinners, because I think your responsibility to your family comes first. It is the woman's responsibility to cook a man dinner and breakfast . . . to keep the house orderly. I wouldn't resent him pitching in once in a while but only once in a while. Let him cut the grass, that's a man's job. If it is a contest between a job and the family, the family should come first. And if you have to quit your job, you just have to quit.

The career-oriented women, on the other hand, do not necessarily de-emphasize the importance of family responsibilities, but many of them envision leaving the tedious aspects of domesticity to household help. One girl who plans to be a lawyer and hopes to marry a lawyer pointed out:

> Obviously things like decorating the house, doing your own cooking, raising the kids, you have to do that yourself. That is something you stamp your own individuality on. But if it is just a matter of making beds, sweeping the floors, or doing the dishes, for that you can get a hired person. I don't think I would be hurting the kids that way, not if I were home when they were.

What Does "Deviance" Mean?

Although the deviance interpretation does not grossly exag-
gerate the research studies from which it was derived, it raises
many questions. Does the deviance notion apply to the whole
range of career-oriented women, all the way from the "career
at any cost" to "career if and when it's convenient"? How
can this view account for women's virtually unanimous desire
to be married and have children? Is it prudent to argue that
the deviant *content* of a young woman's ambitions necessarily stems from "abnormal" personality characteristics? Society's values do stamp strong career aspirations as different,
unusual, at variance with accepted standards, but less and less
so; and this does not mean that the person who has such
plans is herself abnormal, maladjusted or conflicted.

The negative slant of the deviance hypothesis contrasts
sharply with the enrichment view, which places career
planning and occupational choice within the context of role
learning and projects positive inducements for turning toward
career. In the enrichment hypothesis, career is not a solution
to personal conflict but a positive choice growing out of
differential learning situations and influences from important
reference groups.

Sex role learning is indeed a basic aspect of socialization.
Our findings imply that there is no single acceptable version
of the female role, and that significant variations occur in sex
role learning. The prevalent view of career women as deviant
hinges largely on women scientists, engineers, physicians,
lawyers—the types who attained advanced degrees, and who,
in earlier times, often remained single and committed
themselves to career first. These are indeed a minority at one
end of the continuum. Even for women engineers, Perrucci
(1970) shows how they arrange and order their lives to
accommodate professional plans. The fact that these women
are so rare testifies to the difficulty of maintaining both
family and career interests. But statistical infrequency should

not be confused with deviancy. After all, geniuses are deviants in the statistical sense, too.

It may be misleading to counterpose the deviance and enrichment approaches. Our intention is to highlight the narrow and negative cast of the deviance view. It has led to an imbalance in applying notions of social mobility to women. Why should a depriving family milieu be associated with career aspirations more strongly for women than for men? For men to choose a high-level career, to do well and to have high aspirations are the normal, accepted things. Men who achieve and strive to achieve are merely fulfilling the American dream. For women, on the other hand, to desire professional training and high achievement and to have intense career orientations are considered unconventional and problematic.

Although our results bolster the enrichment explanation, the deviance variables are not excluded entirely. Early socialization encourages girls to please others, but boys to achieve. The irony comes from behavioral scientists' tendency to judge conflicted family relationships as conducive to a positive outcome (achievement) for males while the same outcome is considered negative for females. Hoffman (1972) presents the matter differently in her review of childhood experiences and achievement. She suggests that a girl needs more encouragement for exploration and independence, more pressure for separating herself from her mother, and perhaps even greater mother-child conflict and maternal rejection.

We speculate that current changes in life styles for both men and women will yield more males with affiliative orientations and more females with achievement orientations. One observer of the changing sex-role scene believes that "young women have apparently been sold on . . . planning for marriage *and* work, and interest in a career can no longer be attributed to a tiny, deviant minority" (Helson, 1972, p. 37). The 1972 study of Stanford University women presents empirical testimony for such a belief. A comparison of 1965 with 1972 students reveals that Stanford undergraduate women have increased radically in their plans to work when their children are under six, and in their definite long-range plans to become doctors, lawyers, professors and scientists. "Graduating men and women now have very similar educational and occupational aspirations" (Stanford Committee, 1972). Still, we are not naïve enough to expect that there are many women or men who can develop the fierce persistence, the intense striving and the focused intellectuality characteristic of these professions, especially the scientific fields (Rossi, 1965). As Bardwick so poignantly summarizes the problem: "significant changes in role participation will require significant changes in the socialization of our youth (of both sexes) and in most if not all of our cultural institutions" (Bardwick, 1972, p. 50).

From our study, the career aspirers emerge as emancipated women, equalitarian in outlook about domestic life. They expect to marry and have children as do their classmates, but they feel at least partly expendable from child-rearing chores. They expect husbands to share the household tasks, including child-care, cooking and cleaning. In that sense, they are "modern" rather than "traditional" in sex-role conceptions.

Although we could conclude that in sex-role conceptions, role models, occupational choice and work values, the career oriented are unconventional or unusual, this is a far cry from concluding that they are deviant, maladjusted or socially solitary. The very definition of career and non-career orientation in this research militates against such a drastic conclusion. Manifest instead is the possibility that career-salient girls were seminally influenced by broad-ranging, varied persons and experiences before and during college to recognize their personal competence and to seek adult roles that would permit its expression. Career aspirers look like beneficiaries of stimulating, variegated environments in which women's roles encompass broad scope and flexible opportunities.

10 Female Futures and Educational Policy

This study began with the expectation that over the four years of college women would cultivate career aspirations. After reviewing our own research results and assessing the findings of many other behavioral science experts, we are convinced that the matter is more complex. Yes, work interests do grow and some career plans begin. But there is little certainty and scant direction toward a life-style commitment to career. However, we uncovered important influences that serve to move some women toward career plans. In this chapter, we will highlight the results presented throughout the book. Then we will discuss the costs and benefits to women of a contingency orientation, as well as the likely impact of feminism on women's career interests. Next, we will suggest ways for encouraging career aspirations in college women.

What can be done to develop rather than discourage, to foster rather than stifle women's full potential? We cannot consider all of the many possible social policies affecting women as do Dahlstrom (1971) and Safilios-Rothschild (1974). Rather, we focus on how to encourage career achievement in women. We dare not leave the reader resigned to accept our rather pessimistic conclusion that women finish college burdened by the societal pressures with which they entered because, on the optimistic side, we found evidence that there are special contexts and people who encourage women to develop career plans. Thus, after summarizing the main points, we will offer strategies for cultivating women's career interests through three key policy sources: first, young women themselves, for they can break the existing barriers to careers; second, those who counsel young women, especially high school and college counselors, but also parents, as they are constant counselors of their daughters; and third, colleges, their faculty, departments and programs.

Highlights of the Book

This book is both a prologue to and a product of the Women's Liberation Movement. It shows why the movement was a necessary instrument for overcoming the barriers to women's careers. But the evidence from national trends and the research on women's role development reveal that, while much progress is now occurring, sizeable obstacles still remain. The college women of the late 1960s reflected the dilemma of educated women, a dilemma now somewhat ameliorated but still prevailing. It is the dilemma of how to combine and juggle the pulls of home and career.

We described the college experiences of one class of women, showing the change and development of their life-style aspirations. These were students in the women's college of a rather small, private, professionally oriented university in the mid-1960s. Both by its curricular offerings and its reputation, the university tended to attract students seeking occupational preparation. Because of this feature, we studied one class of women intensively through questionnaires and interviews to ascertain their preferences and plans for later life, involving educational, occupational and familial goals.

Our study concentrates on the college years and the plans that students make year by year. The data feature attitudes and intentions rather than actual career choice. We intend to survey the study class to ascertain their life styles as adults after college and to determine what choices.they made in the realms of education, work and family. Unfortunately, the follow-up is still in the future. Readers are reminded that this book presents research on women's role development and career aspirations *during* college.

We found that the women generally make greater steps toward graduate school, toward deciding on an occupation and working at some time after college. In other words, their potential to pursue careers grows. The irony, however, is that these women vary and waver in their ideas about adult life. Most seek an interesting life with room for advanced education, work, a husband, children, perhaps leisure, travel and hobbies. Unlike the narrowing of occupational choice typical of male students, they pursue a contingency approach, remaining open and shifting—not ready to commit themselves to a binding blueprint. Work plays a clear part for them. They hope to find an interesting job, preferably at a professional level. Mainly, however, they expect to tie work around family exigencies—husband, children, economic pressures will dictate either the woman's need to work or her freedom to seek it. Thus, these women are rather conventional in building their lives around family. They are even conventional when they specify an occupation because they opt mainly for typical women's fields; few gravitate toward medicine, law, journalism or scientific research.

A further finding concerns the amount and timing of changes in these role aspirations. Great changeability is typical. The period of greatest change in occupational choice is unquestionably freshman year. But the time between junior and senior years is noteworthy for shifts in career salience. A great spurt occurs at that time toward interest in combining work with family life. Between freshman and junior years, there are gradual rather than abrupt shifts in aspirations.

What appeared as a rather homogeneous class of upper

middle-class white women turned out to be rather diverse. There are not merely the career oriented and non-career oriented. Rather, five types emerge, if one considers the patterns of change and consistency in life-style aspirations each of the four years. There are:

• Careerists, the consistent career aspirers who want to combine career with family roles

• Non-careerists, oriented primarily to family roles with some work and leisure pursuits

• Converts to career aspirations, who begin college without such interests but move toward career by sophomore, junior or senior years

• Defectors, who are career oriented as freshmen and even after but shift to domestic concerns by senior year

• Shifters, who are changeable and inconsistent, whose aspirations vary from year to year, lacking clear-cut direction. Despite this variation, the non-careerists predominate in the study class; consistent careerists and converts to career comprise only 40 percent of the class. It is the non-careerists, defectors from career and shifters who predominate.

Both the preponderately conventional aspirations and the great shifting suggest how rare and difficult career choices remain even for college-educated women.

Women fail to fit common theories about occupational choice because they do not merely seek a field of work. Instead, they worry about meshing work with other features of womanhood, features hard to predict. Will she marry, what kind of husband will he be, will there be children, what should she want to accomplish in life? These remain the unknowns that foster the contingency strategy, the waiting, watching, and wondering what to do. Partly because of these concerns, choices of occupation reflect notions about "what is suitable for a woman" rather than interests and abilities. For such reasons educated women also find it tough to crystallize and specify which field to pursue.

A variety of sources seem to influence these young

women. Family background and experiences in the work world and in college all play a part. The students who are not career oriented more often join sorority and go steady by senior year, their mothers tend to pursue leisure activities and volunteer work. Career-oriented women value work that allows using their special abilities and more likely choose male-dominated occupations; they more often are Jewish and have working mothers; they themselves have more work experience and feel their occupational choice has been influenced by people such as teachers, professors, counselors and others, rather than by family.

Two important influence processes appear to be at work. First, the career-oriented women are exposed to a wide variety of possible role models—their own mothers, their male and female peers, and people in various occupations. Women can more readily perceive themselves in careers when those around them demonstrate that occupation is an important personal commitment. Others serve as reference groups by showing how to perform in a specific occupation. And more importantly for women, when these significant others are female, they explicate how a woman can play several central life roles; for example, by being both a mother and a professor. By contrast, for the non-career oriented, strong influences come from reference groups supportive of traditional sex roles—sorority is a striking example of such influence, but so are their homemaker mothers and their boyfriends. While career and non-career aspirers share role models such as mothers and peers, the content of the influence differs.

The second important influence process refers to more general environmental socialization. Career women have different experiences in growing up, experiences that stress wider options and life possibilities. Career-salient women, while statistically unusual, still are not behaviorally deviant or maladjusted. Rather, they have experienced enriching environments at home, at school and through jobs that reveal multiple options for a woman's adult life. Through such broadening rather than conventional socialization, career becomes a viable commitment for a young woman.

Why Career?

We readily confess the bias that underlies this study: that women ought to seek careers. But we mean more than that simplistic statement. We believe in greater options and opportunities than women now either have or want to exercise. Let women ask themselves, "Who am I"—but more than that, let them learn "What can I become?"

Of course, it is now *possible* for those who wish careers to seek them—but at great personal and social cost. Few women make it. The career-bound woman today has to overcome and circumvent obstacles, not least of which is the conventional wisdom about the educated woman's life style. We can see from the study class that many women fail to consider career at all before and during college, others consider it then drop the idea, and still others simply vacillate. Strategies for making career feasible will need to affect girls with career interests long before they reach college. To facilitate career aspirations calls for altering basic societal values, including the growing-up process.

And preparation for both work and life is sheer realism. More and more educated women work and want to work. Cultivation of career interests during college can lead to an intelligent occupational choice and to a meaningful life plan. Now the lack of "tooling up" precipitates women into the confusion and desparation of middle age—with children grown and husbands occupied there is emptiness, uselessness and searching. Inevitably, bright and educable women feel stupid and stultified, willing to settle for distraction and diversion rather than challenge and stimulation. Though many try and a few succeed, it is hard to start life at forty, no matter what the adage says.

There can be no guarantees to last an entire lifetime. But the costs of women's unadulterated contingency orientation are great.

The Costs and Benefits of Contingency

Women learn early to fit the pattern of flexibility, resiliency and responsiveness to others. It becomes so well ingrained that by adulthood unlearning the contingency approach to life is difficult for most, impossible for many. Yet a contingency conception of life has important benefits. Among other things, it reminds us that role conflict is not inevitable, that people are more malleable and can more readily reconcile diverse demands than even behavioral scientists assumed, and it reveals how adaptive human beings can be (March, 1972). Above all, it is clear that men have benefited greatly from their mothers and wives who deferred self-interest to family interest or negated self-interest entirely, or perhaps even equated the two. Women's absorption in launching their menfolk provided some side benefits, of course. There was excitement in the varying stages through which children pass with their trials and tribulations, there was the elevation over the protégé's success, the pleasure in reflected glory: "I am John Smith's mother" or "I am Mrs. John Smith" as the case may be. The biggest benefit of all was the woman's successful avoidance of the risks in trying to achieve herself.

As economists well know, however, there are no benefits without costs. The costs to women personally and the social costs of wifeship and motherhood are far from trivial—and they seem to have grown greater, the more sensitized we become to available alternatives (Bernard, 1972). Putting her own preferences last, the woman typically delayed her own development—even pursuit of hobbies like painting or weaving got the lowest priority with the rationalization: "I'll do more when the children are older. . . ." Pursuing a profession might be put out of mind with the conviction that "I can never give it the time and effort necessary to succeed." One can easily conclude that woman was her own worst enemy, fearing to stretch herself, unwilling to test the firmness of sex-role definitions, reluctant to try and compete.

The result of putting one's self last has carried with it some awesome penalties for many women: (1) a pattern of avoiding achievement in education, work or community life, thus effectively making the top artistic and professional fields unattainable (Horner, 1972); (2) settling for less recognition, less money, less prestige in the arenas that women do enter; (3) fostering some "trained incapacities" (Burke, 1954) to concentrate for long periods, to conduct sustained activity, to listen carefully, to speak self-confidently; (4) developing some serious personality deficiencies like "self-hatred," condemnation of other women, and low self-esteem (Broverman, et. al., 1972; Frieze, 1974; Toews, 1972). The costs boil down to wasted human resources both for the individuals involved and for the society at large (Cross, 1973).

There is still another way to assess the contingency approach that pertains less to the role differences between men and women and more to the life-style benefits for both sexes in a highly changeable world. Adapting to change is a key life exigency these days—one demanded increasingly from everyone: thus men can begin to benefit from flexibility in adjusting to alterations in economic conditions and career opportunities. Men can consider mid-career changes more readily, pursuing new occupations and new life patterns akin to what women have been doing after children grow up. Experimentation with marriage forms and variant life styles takes flexibility and accommodation to others. Men may contemplate the satisfaction of wives who are fulfilled instead of constantly responding to excessive pressures for their own achievement. Fathers and husbands may discover the pleasures of greater leisure time and more family life. Educated men already seem more prepared to accommodate their work plans to those of their wives—they show a greater interest in the woman's earning capacity, her independence and pursuit of her own career (Almquist, 1974).

The Feminist Movement and Women's Careers

The initial fears aroused by the Women's Liberation Movement have subsided. Feminism dramatically highlighted the dilemmas experienced quietly by women of all ages. The movement exposes problems perceived even by non-liberated women.

On the positive side, it has capitalized on existing trends that now free women for choosing alternatives formerly unavailable. Birth control technology, which facilitates smaller families and child-free marriages; women's accelerating push into the labor force; ingenious household appliances that minimize the drudgery of housework; civil rights legislation that recognizes women's need for abortion services; laws that distribute the financial resources and liabilities (the children) more equitably between divorcing spouses; men's rather recent disenchantment with war, work and the success dream; the sexuality revolution with its mixture of openness, variety and recreation—all these rebound to the cause of liberation for both men and women.

In turn, feminists have encouraged role choices for both sexes: legislatively through their push for equal educational and employment opportunities, for basic human rights; in the family sphere, by stress on men's involvement with pregnancy, childbirth and child-care and for day-care services; in education, by exposing sexist children's literature and boosting women's studies right into academe. All these promise to alter female self-concepts and foster men's acceptance of women as equals.

But how radical will these changes look ten years from now? Will the "new" developments take root and grow? On the negative side, we suspect that feminism is not and cannot be enough. Though it may aspire to such heights, no social movement can be a panacea. It creates some new problems while "solving" some old ones, and some key problems still persist. Marriage and motherhood remain as popular and pervasive as before—they are merely modified by the shorter time commitments resulting from earlier childbearing, smaller families and higher divorce rates.

As long as women are *mainly* responsible for child-rearing and for family life, the contingency approach will dominate their lives, especially the self-denial, the acquiescence to others and the responsibility for children's well-being. The working mother has to arrange for child-care; even when she leaves home, the mother must oversee household and family affairs (Lave and Angrist, 1974). Since raising children is challenging and difficult, mothers find it strenuous to combine work, play and family. Juggling is a rare skill that takes perfecting. As the vernacular goes, "keeping all the balls in the air is not easy," and dropping a ball or two is a constant risk. Women's deeply ingrained passivity and men's stubborn assertiveness may continue to seduce women away from career aspirations and high achievement.

As an alternative to juggling several difficult roles, women will need to find a behavioral style other than contingency orientation. To achieve professionally—to attain recognition —calls for a dedication to work and a setting of priorities unfamiliar to some women and uncomfortable to many. In these realms, men tend to be the role models, with accompanying "masculine" behavioral styles. The aspiring woman has to answer the male's question: "Why can't you be like me?" She has to learn dominance, competition and mastery with the concomitant danger of ridicule for lack of feminity.

Structural changes in the economy and labor force projections add dimensions of doubt about the future for women's career aspirations (Manpower Report, 1973). Just as women's appetite for work mushrooms, there is a growing interest in a shorter work week combined with a rise in leisure activities, both of which move men away from the occupational sphere. Women's nascent career aspirations must face discouragement by men's declining work involvement. But more than that, serious retractions in demand are projected in the top professions, such as medicine, law, college teaching and scientific research. In addition, the traditional women's fields—nursing, teaching, library science and social work—are already experiencing sharply reduced job opportunities. Together with the adverse effects on women workers of periodic recessions and spurts in unemployment, economic conditions are far from conducive to implementing the fondest hopes of liberated careerists (Gold, 1973).

The lesson from other countries and contexts also augers caution. In the Soviet Union, where most women work, few of them attain high government posts. The many women physicians and engineers are supervised by male colleagues. And working mothers at all occupational levels drudge unaided in the house both before and after the work day (Epstein, 1970). In Sweden, efforts to emancipate women continue with special emphasis on legal mechanisms. Enforcing behavioral changes has not been as easy as expounding equalitarian ideas. Among proposed laws, one would call for universal child-care services and, another, individual rather than spousal income tax liability (Dahlstrom, 1970). The Israeli kibbutz was the original harbinger of women's equality, free love and work assignments based on collective roles. Increasingly, kibbutz ideologues and ordinary members alike debate and sometimes yearn for parental child-rearing and more family involvement. Contemporary kibbutz women tend to fill sex-typed jobs, to have less administrative responsibility and to feel more dissatisfied with their life on the kibbutz than men (Rabin, 1970). Contemporary American communal experiments represent a wide range of sexual and familial arrangements, but many of them boast of rigid sex-role distinctions with an ultra-traditional role for women: subservience to men, premarital chastity, strict monogamy and full child-care responsibility (Roberts, 1971). Since communal societies remain unusual and experimental, even established ones like the kibbutz must struggle to survive, and in so doing they are well served to glorify motherhood.

Although we urge our readers to heed the forces that slow equality for women, we argue that women's agility and flexibility combined with planning can encourage career aspirations. While we do not offer the "compleat" guidebook for rearing such life planners, we can suggest ways for fostering career commitment.

What College Women Can Do

In our longstanding roles as college professors we counsel women students far more often than we advise others on how to counsel women. So telling college women how they can pursue careers is an easier task than addressing their elders or their significant others. And it is fitting to bring this book to a close by addressing the very women and their successors who made this study possible. We take special satisfaction in building the advice on what we learned from the students themselves. We stress particularly those conditions that facilitate career aspirations, even though we recognize that many college women will continue to prefer a "job" rather than a "career." Our concern is that educated young women know clearly what alternatives they have so that they can try creative combinations of these alternatives. We underscore here, as throughout this book, what this study brought home to us—that choosing an occupation and planning a career are part of a total life configuration. The educated person who takes short-term goals like holding a job or marrying or having children as a full life plan is deliberately myopic.

Since what went before in this chapter is closely tied to what comes next, we urge our women student readers to bear with us and read the whole chapter through. Then our aims will be obvious: to look for system changes as well as individual changes; to expect that the total life view will affect college curricula; to presume that teachers, counselors, parents, peers and husbands will help open up alternatives; to anticipate that colleges will create enriching environments including significant role models for women students. And for the young woman herself, our aims are that she exploit all the resources in the college environment and that she develop her full potential.

Exploiting Educational Resources

There is much more to college than just classwork. Every student knows this. But women often settle for less. They use too little of the available resources. They let questions go unanswered, they stay silent in class discussion, they struggle with confusing and meaningless curricula. It takes courage to uncover the resources that exist, it takes heroics to create resources where there are none. What we advocate is stretching and bending the system so that it will yield the intellectual and personal fruits students deserve.

The most obvious reward schools offer is getting good grades. Women do well at achieving grades—that is the most routinized element of academic achievement in college. Grades are the currency of academia (Becker et. al., 1968), rather easy to accomplish if one follows the rules and the lore about taking tests and writing papers.

More challenging, though less obvious, are the opportunities for intellectual development, for learning professional values, for exercising personal preferences, for testing skills and abilities. These opportunities exist in a variety of forms during college. The student can ask questions during and after class of the professor in order to clarify ideas or solve problems that arise in the class. She can make a deliberate effort to do the homework and come well prepared for discussion in classes that utilize student participation. There can be no excuse then for silence and for holding back when all around vocal and sometimes ignorant males spout their views and dominate the discussion. The student who knows the material and gives tangible evidence of her brightness to faculty members will reap a harvest—she will find professors interested in her ideas, eager to answer questions, ready to direct her to further information, and above all willing to get to know her. This personal knowledge and respect for the able student leads the professor to suggest departmental projects on which she can work part-time or in the summer, and to give recommendations to employers and graduate schools. Even if not sought out, she can seek contact with faculty through asking for part-time and summer jobs, and asking questions.

By joining or organizing a departmental club, the student learns to know her classmates in the same field. She gets to "talk shop" about classes, professors, work plans and personal views. The professional club creates access to faculty as well as students, to practicing professionals as well as to apprentices. So it can lead to work opportunities both on campus and off, and to role models who show how they carry out their professional and life roles.

Willingness to explore and tap existing resources can yield rewards in getting to know one's self. The woman can discover how competent she is in dealing with people, tasks and ideas. The student who seeks out knowledgeable people —older students, administrators, professors in other fields, people in the community—to answer her questions may find that she is capable in dealing with people, flexible in learning strategies and open to new ideas. Work experiences may reveal that her field choice is wrong and must be changed. Or she may discover that rules are elastic, not totally fixed; that other people can bend to her needs as well as she to theirs; that the field is not rigid but has room for her interpretation of it.

Developing One's Full Potential

It is no longer sufficient to be a woman or a man. It is the whole person with full human potential that counts. As Polonius said to his son, "To thine own self be true," so we say to our spiritual daughters, "Follow your abilities and inclinations." The sense of one's self as a person cannot come wholly from others' definitions, for that is life by default. The woman who wants a career must rely on herself to make the dream a reality. She must lead, not follow; she can choose, not wait to be chosen. There continue to be strong forces that hold women back, through habit and inertia, through intention and discrimination. Women's own reluctance to achieve is a supreme restraint difficult to break. To overcome these forces takes a momentum wrought from hard work, clear goals and a broad conception of life.

The woman who wants work to be a central life fulfillment has to hold that aim constantly before her. Her life will be more than a home, a sex partner and children; her life will be more than yielding to others. Her life will be assertion of self, her life will be stamped with her ambitions and interests, with her abilities and aspirations. She will want to be launched rather than just launching others, she will turn fantasies of achievement into fights for recognitions, she will barter hesitation for striving, she will trade silence for success.

What Counselors and Parents Can Do

Many people can potentially influence women's choices and their views of what life offers. Ordinarily, vocational counselors have had the special task of helping young people discover and define their interests. But our study emphasizes the importance of *all* adults who counsel the young—parents, teachers, professors, counselors, co-workers. This section is, therefore, addressed to all who advise girls during high school and college, both official "counselors" and unofficial ones. We offer two ways in which such counseling should be presented to women: first, as a total life view with planning for adulthood rather than mere selection of an occupation, and second, the presentation of alternatives available in the work world, moving away from narrow field definitions and from sex-typing to wider options.

Stressing the Total Life View

If the economy continues to expand, the demand for women workers will continue. "More married women are working today than ever before in our history because there are economic opportunities for them to do so" (Rossi, 1967). But indications of a decline in the fertility rate with a slower growth rate of the economy will yield fewer children to teach and less demand for workers of all kinds (Gold, 1973). Add to this the occasional economic recession and automation of many jobs (computerized instruction, diagnosis, and information retrieval in teaching, nursing and library work, respectively). With such job shrinkage, especially in the traditionally female fields, are women misled to seek careers? No. They may be joined increasingly at home, in leisure activities, and in volunteer work by their men. Both sexes may then be liberated from work. Some men have already "learned to be as adaptable and responsive as most women" (Riesman, 1973). Men especially will need to know how to live meaningful lives without paid work. To be liberated will then mean to be free to choose from among many options of which a gainful career is only one alternative. Guidance counselors will have to sketch out such broad alternatives so that young people's future plans glimpse the whole spectrum of possibilities. To live in a changing world, contingency planning will become the norm. Instead of falling into the hazards of life's stages by not planning, they will have to make the contingencies explicit and important rather than vague and trivial.

In our study, it is clear that the most dramatic shifts in student behavior occurred between high school and sophomore year. So it is the freshman stage in which students are most affected by the college environment. Secondarily, the last year is a time of marked change but not nearly so much as the first year. College as a change agent is operative at the beginning and the end. Many studies of college students corroborate this special feature of the two stages (Feldman and Newcomb, 1969, Chapter 4). Freshman year involves the experience of newness, adjustment to college life, some disillusionment in precollege expectations. Despite these, the first year is one of excitement. Senior year has the specialness of a finale, a disengagement from the institution and very often from student status. Counselors should be particularly sensitive to freshmen concerned about choice of major and to beginning seniors groping for what to do after college. Perhaps intervention at these two stages can be most influential in helping students make intelligent choices.

The great variability observed, even in the fairly homogeneous woman's college studied, shows that we cannot expect the same effects in all (or even most) students. *Some* people change in *some* ways: in life-style aspirations, noticeable numbers moved in opposite directions, both to and from career orientation! Unlike the total institution such as prison or military school, college encourages change but does not force it. It certainly fails to result in a predominant and explicit prototype. In this sense, to educate is to produce an open-ended rather than a defined product, a variety of products rather than a single product. A criterion of the counselor's impact might be that students take stock of themselves. Students pointed out during the interviews that taking part in the research pushed them to answer questions about themselves, to reflect on their opinions and plans. Should not the daily exposure to ideas, people and situations have at least that consequence? Certainly, the fact that study participants perceived themselves as changed by senior year suggests that even if radical objective changes were not evident, college itself makes people *feel* different. Counselors can capitalize on student concerns with self-development, encourage their desire to plan for life and help them sort out personal goals.

Presenting Alternatives

In vocational counseling, there is a dire need to clarify ossified notions about occupational choice. Myths about women's work, men's work, child-rearing and leisure persist. Young women are heir to these societal stereotypes. For example, the idea that women's fields are "secure" or "practical" choices imply that a teacher, nurse, or librarian can "always find a job" and leave to re-enter her field after a ten-year lapse without becoming obsolete. No professional field, "women's" or "men's," can be safe in this unchanging way any longer. This view is false and unprofessional, and it belittles the fields it describes.

The idea that "women's fields" permit working short hours or flexible convenient schedules does not always hold up to fact. Nurses may work night shifts and department-store buyers have a six-day week. On the other hand, the physician or architect may work part-time or even only part of the year. Yet the entire work world is built around the concept of the 40-hour week, the full-time job, the permanent employee. The widespread occurrence of part-time and temporary jobs is nevertheless viewed as unusual, an exceptional arrangement. It falls on each woman who wants to avoid the standard work week to carve out a schedule and negotiate to obtain it. The expanding emphasis on leisure and the shrinking demand for workers have already altered the work pattern in some skilled occupations. Some of the professionals may follow suit, redounding to women's benefit as well as men's. But until the rigid time structure in most jobs is modified, women will continue to pay the penalties for convenience: lower wages, no retirement or medical benefits, no seniority or promotion. They may go on accepting the male myths and definitions pervasive in the work world.

The counselor can stress that occupational choice should be made in order to fulfill one's individual potential, not merely to earn a livelihood or to be practical. Counselors also have to question and even abandon existing vocational preference tests which segregate male and female occupations by using different population norms and separate test forms. Such a practice perpetuates outdated and unacceptable sex role stereotypes in work choices. Counselors must help end the circular process by which "women discover and assert their gender by their choices" of fields and these fields "take on a feminine character because they are chosen by women or rejected by men" (Hall, 1964; Useem, 1966).

Opening up alternatives for women can come through identifying potential role models and making them explicit. The role models for a girl can range from parents to friends to teachers. All of these are important. The mother sets an example in her emphasis on leisure or work or both. If a mother works while the girl is growing up, she shows that job-holding is acceptable and manageable for a woman with family responsibilities. She may even show that work is stimulating and enjoyable.

In addition to pointing out role models, counselors have to counteract the fictions that still color women's views. To parallel the man-made myths about work, women perpetuate their own myths about domesticity and child-care; the fiction that child-care and homemaking are unimportant has helped the woman derogate herself as "just a housewife." While she is expected to consider these responsibilities as desirable for herself and her family, these are seen as duty not pleasure, as obligation not contribution. It is the extra-household work that is exciting, not the cooking, cleaning and childcare.

Unless counselors and important adults appreciate the challenges inherent in child-rearing, and the benefits of successful child-rearing not only to children but to parents and to society as a whole, women will continue to be dutiful domestic drones. The rising fear of today's wayward youth with its drug, delinquency, restiveness and sex problems may lead us to re-examine the crucial socialization process. Economic criteria are inadequate to estimate the social costs and benefits of what adults can do. The equation that includes what men and women contribute to society has to put a value on child-rearing and on other unpaid work as well as on gainful employment, and for both sexes.

What Colleges Can Do

Students welcome the potential for personal development offered in the college context. The educational benefits touted as the promise of university education are taken as the student legacy regardless of sex. But women have to unravel the contradiction (or perhaps merely contend with it) between the educational goal with its centrality of personal-intellectual growth and the societal goal they brought to college for the woman to be an activator, a launcher of husband and children but not of herself. In the study class, only the consistently career oriented can reconcile these two goals; the others simply accept the conventional roles in their life script. And this prevails despite the current images of educated women as independent, sexually free and participants in the labor force and marriage as democratic and equalitarian. Because paralleling this emancipated view is the image of women as glamorous, leisure oriented and family centered, which highlights the need to please and guide others. Thus, the sex-role dilemmas girls heard about in high school hover during college and re-emerge afterward.

Two strategies can intrude on these dilemmas and minimize them: (1) the more general one of creating an enriched environment and welcoming women into it and (2) the more specific one of providing role models.

Enriching the Environment

The main vehicles for enhancing the university's influence on women are the programs, majors, curricula, fields and departments. If these elements are to be meaningful to women, they must reflect the stance that education is preparation not only for work but for life. Nor do we mean the once-common idea that a woman's life is home and hearth. That led to the onerous sex-segregated curricula that channel women into "women's" fields and men into "men's" fields. Invariably, the assumptions were that men's fields are superior to women's and that males and females lead totally distinctive adult lives. These assumptions justified lower expenditures for women's fields in many universities, second-class status for the coordinate women's colleges and unique but lesser prestige even of the elite Eastern women's colleges.

Many educators express ambivalence about the disappearance of women's colleges (Riesman, 1973). And rightly so. The argument has always been that a separate educational arena best prepares women to perform intellectually and personally in the world. While the elite "Seven Sisters" colleges have always ranked high academically, their strength comes more from the independent liberal arts college context they offer than from being women's colleges. As Stern (1970) reports, the aristocratic women's colleges share with the co-educational small private liberal arts institutions high intellectuality, high achievement orientation and individual assertiveness among students. Both the women and men at these schools exceed most other college students in intellectuality and social aggressiveness. Since the coed liberal arts colleges have approximately as many females as male students, both sexes seem to contribute equally to creating and sustaining the intellectual culture. Thus, despite some real educational benefits of the good women's colleges, there is no evidence that they offer *unique* educational advantages. Furthermore, the adult world is *not* sex-segregated and it *is* highly competitive. Isolating women from the real world, even temporarily, has condoned their low status rather than elevating them as peers in the world of the educated classes—they become the wives of the successful, but hardly successful in fulfilling themselves.

Sex-segregated education reinforces not merely women's special qualities; tragically, it underscores women's lower value in society. It buttresses the view that family is a trivial matter not important enough for men, and it perpetuates the sex-typing of occupations. Ironically, "women's" fields like teaching continue to emphasize behavior "suitable for a woman," to minimize professionalism and to channel women back into "woman's place" instead of forward into the world. The difficulty for women these days is that the dying women's colleges and the "phased-out" women's fields have not been replaced with equally attractive, elite and practical alternatives.

Only when institutions of higher education discard restrictive condescending assumptions and adopt new assumptions based on bringing women in at all levels and in all fields can they expect to foster female careerists. The new stance calls for helping people learn to learn, to prepare for life as well as work, to facilitate development. It requires shifting from domains of masculinity and femininity to broader conceptions of life.

Openness of this sort includes structural adaptations such as part-time study and continuing education. These will fit both women and men better for a changing unpredictable world and, in fact, are growing in popularity. So will wider curricular offerings suit both sexes for life. Neither men nor women have the continuity between generations once taken for granted. Parenthood and spouseship are not the obvious things they used to be.

What is effective child-rearing? What is a happy marriage? What is a satisfying relationship? These are constant questions little answered either by "natural" sex-tied skills or by inherited doctrine. In these matters, the behavioral sciences can provide some answers to some questions. We now know much about the nature of learning and development, interpersonal relations, the consequences of various child-rearing techniques, of varying marital patterns, about contraception and sexuality. The time has come for young people to learn about these matters explicitly and systematically. As Alice Rossi (1968) argues so well, how to bear and raise children is not a woman's "natural" competence; it has to be learned by women because they are expected to know it. Nor do all women enjoy these responsibilities even while executing them. By this token, both men and women need to be able to make choices to marry or not, to be parents or not. And if yes, both need to learn explicitly what these roles may encompass, beginning in high school and continuing in college. As professionals and as citizens, people can then make choices out of knowledge rather than ignorance. It is in society's interest as well as the individual's.

Providing Role Models

The study class' strong interest in academic professions that either involve college teaching or require graduate school training suggests that students learn to relish being in the university setting, and seek to prolong it either through further education or through their occupational choice. The faculty power to elicit and encourage women in career pursuits, at least in academic fields, is great. When teachers are female, they can do more than merely praising a student for her academic achievement. As women, wives and mothers, they can demonstrate how a professional career articulates with the woman's entire constellation of roles. And regardless of their sex, teachers serve to reward the woman's ability, to encourage her inclinations, to shape her self-image as an able person.

Unless universities recognize and honor faculty women's accomplishments with system rewards, students will continue to believe that they cannot make it either—and they will be accurate. By recruiting, hiring and promoting competent women workers, the institution notifies its women students that high aspirations are rewarded. Special efforts to draw women into men's domains like engineering and sciences should be matched with attempts to attract men into women's realms like elementary school teaching and the arts; and all of this applies to both faculty and students.

Within fields or departments, colleges offer built-in role models when they provide points of contact between faculty and students, or among students within a field. Professional and departmental clubs begin the collegial pattern among peers that grows into professional societies and associations. Opportunities for summer and part-time work experience with faculty members offer the apprenticeship type of learning so crucial to role modeling. But faculty can also facilitate job placement in allied fields during college, so that women see role models in occupations outside academe.

We have studied the problems of career for women, and we have prescribed some remedies. Much is already being done to foster women's career achievement. Yet much more remains to be done. College professors, career counselors, parents and young women must now understand what Eliza Southgate understood so well in 1801:

> Women who have not incentives to action suffer all the strong energetic qualities of the mind to sleep in obscurity. In this dormant state they become enervated and impaired, and at last die for *want of exercise.* . . . The cultivation of the powers we

possess, I have ever thought a privilege—or I may say duty—that belonged to the human species, and not man's exclusive prerogative. (Eliza Southgate Bowne, 1888.)

We hope that the lessons learned by an educated woman six generations ago can be learned again. But more than mere learning, "cultivation of the powers we possess" should become a reality.

Appendix 1: How the Study was Conducted

The Setting

A professional-technical emphasis pervaded the women's college despite its partial segregation from the remainder of the university. The women's college was contained largely within one building, which bore its name. Departmental offices and many faculty offices were centered there, particularly for home economics, business studies, sociology and biology. Most of the humanities faculty were housed in another building as members of an academic division of humanities and social sciences. This division serviced all the undergraduate colleges.

Masculine and feminine endeavors were separated because men could not major in history, English, technical writing, psychology, modern languages or social science. Women students took degrees in precisely these areas but a few pursued B.A. degrees in mathematics, chemistry or physics, thereby taking some courses with male students. While the faculties for these majors were located in a college of engineering and science fields, the degrees were granted from the women's college. Male and female students, then, sometimes mingled in class but seldom participated together as majors in the same programs of study.

When the study began in 1964, the women's college comprised the smallest number and proportion of the undergraduate population with barely one fifth of the undergraduates, while science and engineering students constituted fully half, and the fine arts had somewhat over one quarter of the undergraduates. The other undergraduate colleges had some women—4 percent of the engineering and science students and 38 percent of the fine arts students were females. By 1967, the proportions of women had increased slightly in these two colleges and a few men had begun to register in the women's college in anticipation of the opening of a liberal arts college.

Before the study, the university, including the women's college, had initiated some stocktaking and self-study in preparation for possible changes in organization and purpose (Kirk, 1965). The momentum for change in the university carried with it the growing national concern of the mid-1960s that single-sex colleges were outdated—that women's colleges in particular were remnants of an earlier time when higher education was designed to serve two distinct populations, one male and one female. The inscription on the building rotunda became somewhat embarrassing:

> These are woman's high prerogatives
> To make and inspire the home
> To lessen suffering and increase happiness
> To aid mankind in its upward struggles
> To ennoble and adorn life's work however humble.

In the summer, lush ivy creepers covered the words but during the bare-walled winter, the quaint phrases stood out again.

Several "women's fields," such as library science, social work and pre-nursing, had been phased out over the years. Now talk of entirely abandoning the women's college became prevalent. Arguments for this move included the idea that secretarial studies and home economics were somehow less academic than English, psychology or economics. These fields were occupationally oriented and the graduates of such programs could go right into the work world, yet their degrees were considered more vocational and less professional than degrees awarded in chemistry or the arts.

Eventually the women's college as a distinct entity was eliminated. In a detailed history of the university, one observer notes that this had two major results: "the replacement of practical training by a more liberal concept of education . . . strengthening the humanities and social sciences on campus, and the growth of graduate education . . ." (Burstyn, 1973). One might well view these as goals, the pursuit of which led to the termination of the specifically female programs and the women's college. Overtly, the university was attempting to abandon sex-segregated education, yet the mindset of the institution had continually been on masculine endeavors, and the institution was unable or unwilling to free itself of its masculine image. This was especially clear among those departments (outside the women's college) that had some women students and a scant women faculty. Departments achieved power because of their all-male or predominantly male membership and proved their importance by emphasizing "hard" research, quantitative methods and practical applications, and by flaunting their professional emphasis. All of these projected a masculine image of fields, departments and colleges devoid of women, "softness" or femininity (Burstyn, 1973).

The university structure and environment remained essentially the same during the four years the study class was in school. Only in the last two years did plans to expand the institution's scope gain momentum. Two related developments did occur between the third and fourth years of this study. One involved a name change from "technological institute" to "university," encompassing some expanded research and course offerings at the graduate level. One involved a name change from "technological institute" to "university," implying a shift from an engineering school to a broader focus and encompassing some expanded research and course offerings at the graduate level. It was also at this time that work began on the gradual phasing out of the women's college and the initiation of a coeducational liberal arts college.

One cannot say the study class was greatly affected by these developments. Students graduated under the departmental and college structure in which they began. Still, talk of change was rampant, enthusiasm for the potential of the new undergraduate programs was prevalent, some disillusionment emanated from the women's college students and both positive and negative sentiment existed among the faculty.

The proposed phasing out gave subtle emphasis to the fact that both students and faculty considered the women's college students to be second-class citizens. They were alleged to have lower intelligence and lesser scholarliness, and to lack solid ambition for professional attainment. Based on the mid and late 1960s, the women's college students did have lower college entrance examination board scores than students in engineering fields and were selected differently from students in the arts. Fine-arts students were judged primarily on performance competency, using portfolios or auditions in their respective fields. Their college board scores were typically lower than those of students in the women's college. Engineering and science students had the highest average scores, achieving approximately 700 in the Mathematics Scholastic Achievement Test and close to 600 on the Verbal SAT. By contrast, the women's college required scores in the high 500's on both tests. The study class was representative for the women's college, averaging 578 on the SAT-V and 586 in the SAT-M, with 40 percent of the class scoring over 600 in both subjects. While students from the women's college had high-school grades comparable to the national norms for freshmen reported by the American Council on Education (Panos, Astin and Creager, 1967), they more often chose their college for its academic reputation and were more likely to achieve national merit recognition. Additionally, women's college students more often felt they could do well in several areas such as music, sketching, sports, homemaking and learning a second language than freshmen women at other universities.

Despite their competence relative to college students in general, the tragedy was that the women absorbed a minority-group self-conception. As a numerical minority with high visibility on a predominantly male campus, they were quick to recognize the prevailing stereotypes. They perceived a low evaluation of themselves and reported it back with some bitterness. As early as the spring semester of freshman year, girls told us in their interviews that they were defined by other students on campus as marriage-oriented, as wanting mainly an "MRS. degree," not a baccalaureate, or that they were dismissed academically as being "just interested in social life." Students often referred to the women's college girls as the "Connie Coeds." Indeed, some girls accepted the label and used it almost with ridicule in describing themselves. To be sure, these caricatures exist at other universities, reflecting the stereotyped, low self-images of women that originate in the larger society. We suspect they were slightly stronger at this and at other schools where there is a pronounced separation of men's and women's fields.

While the women's college freshmen had somewhat higher opinions of their contemporaries in the other divisions of the university than of themselves, they downgraded the men's social agility, describing them derisively as "toothpicks with heads on," "skinny engineers with glasses," "baggy pants and worn-out briefcases thinking about some problem in math," "the horn-rimmed boys who have no fun." About fine-arts students, the women said "they are so dedicated, so committed to their work." "Their whole life is performing, working, but they dress rather weird. . . ." On the whole, the college students thought of themselves as middle range among the student assortment, as equilizers and more normal. They thought they were the only group immersed in the liberal arts, which they saw as a central purpose of higher education. As they progressed through their particular majors, becoming absorbed in the technical requirements, they were better able to defend their interests as important, requiring both talent and hard work.

These descriptions of the history and setting are offered in order to provide the background necessary for understanding the particularities surrounding the women who were studied. We turn next to a description of the students themselves.

The Study Class

Just as special images of the women's college existed vis-à-vis the other undergraduate colleges, so too there were prevailing conceptions of the characteristics of the student body. A detailed examination showed the study class as a special blend of several student types, with many social backgrounds represented. The university appeared to attract solidly middle-and upper-class girls from urban areas in the Eastern United States. In point of fact, just over half of the fathers were executives or managers, owners of businesses or professionals. About 45 percent grew up in large cities, with the remainder coming from small towns or suburbs. Most were from outside the metropolitan area, but a substantial one third were from the locality. The predominant pattern both for the locals and the out-of-towners was to live in the dormitories or in apartments surrounding the campus. Still, the commuter element was present, with 15 percent living at home. In religion, the class was nearly evenly divided among Jewish, Protestant and Catholic faiths. Three fourths described their parents as church or synagogue members. Approximately half of the students' mothers had some college; one third were college graduates. Around 40 percent of the students' mothers were employed. This figure is very similar to the proportion of married women who worked in the country as a whole.

Among the larger concerns in student life were campus activities, dating and meeting people. Even though the university was known for high-level scholarship, and in turn students described the university in such terms, the extra-classroom elements of life grew in potency after freshman year. While grades went up, concern over getting good grades declined, and the importance of dating and mating grew as girls increasingly became attached to a boyfriend or fiancé. As freshmen, just over half dated once a week or more often; as seniors, three fourths did so. Sorority membership was very prevalent among the study class. Participation in extra-curricular activities increased each year; as freshmen, about 42 percent described themselves as moderately or very active in college clubs and organizations; by the end of junior year, two thirds of the students were active.

The women's college offered majors in a wide range of fields. The study class began with 188 freshmen distributed so that 31 percent were in the sciences, 27 percent in humanities, 27 percent in home economics and business and 15 percent in social science. In freshman year the largest single major field, proportionately, was English (a few of these students were in technical writing and editing). The lowest proportion of students was in physics. By senior year, the number of science majors dwindled and the physics majors disappeared, mostly through transfer into the engineering and sciences division. The largest declines occurred in the sciences, which comprised only 11 percent of the senior class, with mathematics reflecting the largest decrease. By contrast, the humanities students now comprised 35 percent, but this derived from an increased proportion only of English majors. The applied fields made up 39 percent of senior majors. In the social sciences, between freshman and senior years, the few economics majors dwindled to one student, social studies remained largely unchanged, while psychology gained a little.

The notable absence of an education major masks the importance of this field in choices of major. In the fall of senior year, 37 percent of the class had selected the teaching option, most preparing for high-school teaching. These included students mainly from home economics, English and business studies majors. The interest in education was highlighted early in the students' occupational preferences. Among freshmen, one fifth listed teaching as their occupational choice and one fourth of the seniors did so. The discrepancy between the 37 percent of seniors in the teaching option and the 24 percent who aspired to be teachers suggests that some teacher trainees did not plan to teach.

The professional-vocational orientation of the school served to attract large numbers of women who were drawn to a specific field when they arrived as freshmen. Over half retained the same major during all four years. The remainder reflected the widespread tendency for college students to shift in and out of fields and to do so most heavily early in their college career. Despite the particular features of the institution, the students there made field choices much like those of other college women. Between freshman and senior years, they moved away from the masculine majors like the sciences and more toward traditionally feminine fields like humanities, education and home economics. So, while the women's college attracted vocationally oriented women, it did not seem to draw atypical women bent on male-dominated professions, with the exception of the science majors. One might conclude here that the very offerings set this limitation by featuring women's fields such as home economics and the humanities. Furthermore, the catalog description of the women's college may be instructive:

> The college has formulated its more specific objectives in terms of the obligations society expects the young woman of today to assume and the opportunities for personal fulfillment now available to her. The programs of study are planned to insure that on graduation you have: (1) the depth of understanding in your field of specialization required to secure good initial employment or admission to the graduate school of your choice; (2) the breadth and diversity of knowledge indispensable to a professional career and to a satisfying and creative life in the home and in the community; (3) an awareness of the contribution your college education can make to the important career of marriage and motherhood.

In these respects the university may have pointed students toward "vocations" rather than professions. It may have served to promote a "work when it's necessary and convenient" orientation instead of a drive toward career for its own sake. Further, this offer of an education uniquely suited both for a woman's family life *and* for work may have selectively recruited students who held this conception of appropriate feminine behavior; it may have elicited vocational orientation rather than a more careerist one.

The Research Design

The major strategy used in this research was the panel method involving repeated testing of the same persons at several different time points (Glock, 1955; Kendall, 1954; Lazarsfeld et. al., 1972; Wiggins, 1973). Members of the study class completed a questionnaire every fall semester. A sample of the class was interviewed every spring semester, and in senior year an attempt was made to interview the entire class. Additional student data were obtained from the university records. Taken together, these intensive data provide considerable material from which it is possible to consider each participating student as an individual case, and to track changes for each woman as well as for the class as a whole.

Students were defined as eligible to participate if they were in college full-time and in the same year as the study class. Each year it was necessary to ascertain from university records which students had returned, those who had transferred to another part of the university or left it entirely, and how many students had transferred into the women's college. Nearly all the students who were eligible to participate did so. The refusal rate was consistently low. Only 3 percent of the sophomores and 9 percent of the juniors and seniors either said they did not wish to be involved or simply failed to keep appointments for the research. In this way, the loss of respondents, a potential hazard of the panel method, was largely avoided.

Among the study class, 58 percent of the original 188 freshmen graduated together four years later. This retention rate is typical for the women's college (in the three years preceding the study, retention rates had varied between 55 and 61 percent); but it is slightly higher than for other colleges and universities. The findings in this book are based on the panel of 87 students who went through college years in phase *and* who provided complete questionnaire data all four years. This core group represents 85 percent of the senior class who had been in the college continuously for four years. The remaining students either had incomplete data or had not participated in the research.

Questionnaires

Initially, freshmen comprised a captive audience for the study since the questionnaire was administered to the total class as part of the orientation in the first week of college. In succeeding years, we attempted to administer the questionnaire to the entire class simultaneously, but we were unsuccessful. Instead, we used a more individual approach. Study participants were sent a letter explaining the research and its continuing nature. They were asked to come to an auditorium or classroom for about a one-hour testing session. Although a few came at appointed times, most had to be contacted individually by phone or mail to come to the investigator's office to complete the forms for that year. During senior year we met study participants at registration and set up an appointment at a time suited to each girl. Most forms were completed early in the fall term, but each year several students delayed until the end of the semester. During sophomore, junior and senior years, 97, 89, and 91 percent of each class, respectively, participated in the study.

The questionnaire administered annually permitted repeating questions in order to obtain measures over four time periods. Most questions were of the forced choice variety, but several offered the respondent an opportunity to comment in her own words. In addition, students were encouraged to indicate whether any questions were difficult to answer. A freshman version of the questionnaire was the longest of the four years, since students answered questions about their family background and high-school experiences. Some questions were omitted after both freshman and sophomore years because some respondents saw them as unclear, unanswerable, or personally objectionable. We asked students about their choices of major and occupation and career aspirations; ideas about further education, work after college, marriage and children; impressions of college, course work, peers and teachers; and their attitudes about adult roles. The marginal distributions of responses to each question for the panel of 87 students closely approximate the distributions for the entire class each year. The actual questionnaires and the class distributions may be obtained from the authors.

Interviews

Interviews were held during the first four to six weeks of spring semester each year. The interviewer used a set of questions as a guide; these were open-ended, discussion-type questions. The topics covered were similar each of the four years, and included impressions of courses, the school, major field, dating and social life, campus life and role aspirations. But the freshman questions had to be refined and expanded.

The senior interviews differed from the other three sets in asking additional questions, specifically about occupational choices, possible sources of influence on such choices and plans for after graduation. Each student was also presented with her completed study materials: all questionnaires she had filled out over the four years and the transcript of her previous interview. Students were asked to comment freely on these materials. Not all respondents felt like taking time to peruse them, but many did and a few commented with amazement on their earlier views. We had two purposes in presenting these materials: one was to get the student's reaction to herself—to note whether she had changed and whether she felt her answers had been honest at each stage. The second reason was to provide each participant with an idea of her contribution to the research, to show the data as concrete and tangible, even interesting to the respondent.

The authors conducted interviews with the assistance of a female graduate student who carried out half the freshman interviews. The interviews were scheduled for about 50 minutes' duration so that students could come between class periods. The exact duration, however, varied from a few extremely short ones of 20 minutes to several of one and a half to two hours. For the first three years, sessions were held during daytime but seniors often found it easier to make nighttime appointments, particularly those who were busy with practice-teaching.

Two procedural variations were introduced after freshman year. At that time, interviews were conducted in a small seminar-type classroom in the women's college building. During the last three years, most interviews were held in a small library room of the women's dormitory; it was an informal room with overstuffed chairs and a pleasant atmosphere. The library was also a convenient location for dorm girls who could simply come downstairs from their rooms in time for the interview. Still, commuter students preferred coming to the interviewer's office in the women's college, and whenever this arrangement suited an interviewee it was done. The second change from freshman year was the use of a tape recorder. Initially, the interviewer had to remember verbatim what was said and record it immediately after the interviewee left. This made freshman interview transcripts skeletal, lacking a full record of the respondent's words. Introduction of the tape recorder provided little problem—no one objected seriously to it. Most girls relaxed after the first few minutes and forgot about the machine. But some breathed a sigh of relief if the machine was switched off as they prepared to leave and a few stayed longer to add: "Now that the tape's off, I can say this . . ."

The selection of interviewees was designed to include a sample of the whole class each year. Each girl was contacted for interview once during the first three years, and all were contacted in senior year. For the freshmen, a random sample of 26 percent of the class was selected for interview. In sophomore year, another 29 percent were randomly selected; they comprised one half of those girls not previously interviewed. Among juniors, the 45 percent of the class who had not been interviewed as underclassmen were interviewed. This method yielded interviewee samples representative of the class for a given year.

Freshmen interviewees were very like the total class in social characteristics, such as social class level, home-town location, religion, college major, student's residence, and rank in high-school graduating class. Sophomores and juniors who were interviewed resembled their remaining classmates in comparisons on seven variables, including college major, student's residence, grades, sorority membership, and graduate-school plans. Among juniors, interviewees were found to differ in having a significantly higher frequency of dating than the total class; we do not know whether this is more than a chance result. Interview protocols were subjected to content analysis with categories developed from the four sets of interviews (Stone et. al. 1966). The content analysis categories with frequencies of responses and interview guides may be obtained from the authors.

How Participants Reacted to the Study

In the earlier stages of the research, students were, after all, fresh freshmen. They assumed that to complete questionnaires was a natural part of the novice's test-taking upon coming to college. In fact, they were given to understand then that the women's college was sponsoring the research; this they took to mean that participation in the study was compulsory. By spring of freshman year when some students were contacted for interviews, we explained that participation was voluntary but strongly encouraged by the administration and by the faculty. About this time, questions were raised in sophomore year as to the study's importance. Some students wondered why they should give time and information to the study staff, they worried that questions were too personal, and a few felt that the women's college was coercing them into participating. It became clear then to the investigators that the research would need much explaining, some publicity on the campus and generally more effort to "sell" the study. A key task was to stress the confidentiality of the data, that no one except the research staff had access to study materials, that these had no relation to or bearing on college records, that data were handled anonymously and used only for group analyses.

Intensive efforts were begun in sophomore year to educate and inform the study class about this particular research and about social science research in general. One specific strategy was to publicize the study by informing the college faculty about its details. The senior investigator personally contacted faculty advisors and department heads to explain the study and to ask their help in encouraging specific students to participate. The student newspaper wrote up the research twice during sophomore year. Upon invitation from faculty and student and alumnae groups, the senior investigator gave talks describing the study, its nature and purpose. Specific invitations for such presentations came from the college faculty, women student's honorary and professional societies and dorm counselors. Whenever possible, early results based on specific questions were described in these talks. But mainly the talks were used to arouse interest and to illustrate some of the questions that such research might answer.

Still another way to educate participants in the study's value was to provide as much feedback as possible. A newsletter was sent out once during each of the last three years reporting on the progress of the research, indicating some findings and explaining the ensuing stages of the study. Since one of the investigators was, at the time, carrying on research on alumnae of the women's college, she included some of these results in the newsletters. In addition, participants were encouraged to read the publications stemming from the student and alumnae studies—these reports were available from the investigators. In spring of sophomore and senior years, the study class was invited to a special dinner held in the women's dormitory and sponsored from research funds. At these dinners girls were encouraged to ask questions about the study and to continue their participation in it.

Participants were not paid for their time and effort. But students seemed to value the techniques of rewarding their participation with information and with the special attention of the investigators. The interviews also served as a reward to participants. Students often indicated that they felt questionnaires forced their answers into certain categories, while interviews permitted respondents to use their own words and give their own impressions. While some thought of the questionnaires as interesting and stimulating, many saw filling out forms as a tedious or difficult task. In contrast, they considered interviews as an opportunity to learn more about the investigators and the research, and to air one's ideas about many aspects of the college.

Most students took advantage of the interview situation to ask about the research in detail. Freshmen had few such questions or comments, but as upperclasswomen, students were particularly curious. After sophomore year, offense or fear from the research all but disappeared and reactions were mainly favorable; at the very least participants wanted to learn about the research. About one third of the class expressed the view that the study was interesting and important. Others probed further to inquire how the results would be used, whether there was hope the results would lead to changing the women's college or university, whether the findings would be published. Students often asked to be kept informed of the research conclusions and many made helpful suggestions to amplify or alter the study.

From the high rates of participation and the strong evidence that students provided meaningful and honest information, our efforts to gain student cooperation appear to have been successful. Nevertheless, we were constantly reminded how labor-intensive is the task of obtaining data from people.

How Typical Is the Study Class?

Since this research is built on one class of college women, it is pertinent to ask: How representative are the data collected from these respondents? Could one expect different responses from other samples of women in the same college? And do these students differ appreciably from women in other colleges or universities?

The first question deals with the resemblance between the women in the study class and other women who preceded or followed them in the women's college. One strategy for studying students might be to sample randomly from successive entering classes perhaps for a five- or ten-year period. In this way, the researcher can determine whether there are changes over time in the composition of entering classes, but not whether the college experience itself produces changes in students. Another approach commonly used is to sample representatively from all four classes at a single point in time. With this approach, the researcher cannot be sure whether differences among, say, the freshmen and senior students are due to the impact of college, simple maturation and development, or differing composition of classes due to dropouts and in-transfers. The panel method—repeated study of one cohort of students—is the only method that allows discovery of which changes in attitudes and preferences occur in the same individuals. Concentrating on one class and tracing it through time suggests that it may be viewed as a population per se, not representative of any students but only of those studied. Or the class may be seen as a sample in the sense of being representative of other classes in the college. The onus is to demonstrate that the class is typical.

Evidence that the class is typical of the women's college was derived from an exact comparison with the 1967 class entering the women's college. Mean college board scores in math and verbal achievement tests were closely comparable for 1964 and 1967 freshmen. The distribution of students in major departments did not differ significantly between the two years, but some variation in major field choices is evident. The 1967 freshmen completed the role-study questionnaire in the first week of college, as had their study predecessors. Statistical analysis of the two sets of responses on 19 variables showed that the women in both classes gave similar responses to 16 of those questions. These questions dealt with college major, mother's education, religion, father's occupation, birth position, extracurricular activities and dating in high school, level of studentship in high school, current marital status, preferred educational level for a woman and a man, occupational choices, future willingness to work when there are no children and the husband's salary is inadequate, willingness to work with two or more children when the husband's salary is adequate, preference for work that allows combining career and family, and graduate school plans. On three questions, the two classes differed significantly: the 1967 freshmen valued good grades less, they preferred to marry later, and their mothers were more often working than the mothers of 1964 freshmen. Thus while the two classes were highly similar, both their mothers and the 1967 students themselves began to look less traditional.

Further evidence that the study class resembled the 1967 freshmen stems from the comparison of the latter group's responses with those for national norms on 1967 freshman woman (Panos, Astin and Creager, 1967). We found two things: (1) a close similarity between the 1967 class and the 1964 study class in the same college, and (2) a striking difference between the 1967 women's college class and the national sample. In this college, freshmen differed from their contemporaries at other schools in the following ways: They began college somewhat younger; they were more likely to plan attending graduate school and to major in English, math and social sciences; they were less likely to choose education as a career. They were more often Jewish and less often Protestant; their fathers had higher incomes; and they were more likely to have scholarship aid. In attitudes they more often valued responsibility, being financially well off, contributing to scientific theory, writing and creating works of art, and keeping up with politics than the national sample. The study class was more likely to discuss religion and politics, and they less often thought that married women belonged at home. These findings are comparisons of the study class and the national sample in terms of their average responses only; we reiterate that there is considerable diversity within the study class. For example, not all of the women in this college plan to go to graduate school; only some intend to keep up with politics. While the study class is not significantly different from the national sample on all these characteristics, we recognize that in both time and place, the sample was special and unique. Still, these results have strong face validity to support the selective, private and professional nature of the women's college.

How Reliable Are the Study Data?

Given that the study class is representative of the women's college, and only somewhat different from a national sample of college women, we must ask whether the data obtained are reliable. Do repeated applications of the same data-collection devices produce the same results? Or, if different results are obtained at two time points, are these differences due to real changes on the part of the respondents or do they reflect some flaw in the testing device itself? One approach to establishing reliability of any measuring instrument is to apply the test once and then again a few days or weeks later, and then compare the results of the two administrations. The principle involved is to choose a time interval long enough so that respondents will not clearly recall their first responses but short enough so that no real change is likely to have occurred.

Measuring reliability by the test-retest method is complicated in this study, since the questionnaires were administered at one-year intervals, a time period in which much real change on many of the items was very likely to have occurred. However, as freshmen, students completed a short form of the study questionnaire one month after they had filled out the original long version. From this we were able to ascertain the reliability of several of the most important scales and items. Included, for example, were a set of work value scales (Eyde, 1963). On each of these, students were asked to rank in order six reasons for working after marriage. This was a rather complex task and these items were eventually dropped from the questionnaire. Even so, Pearsonian correlation coefficients between these tests one month apart ranged from .61 to .73 for 185 freshmen.

A key dependent variable on this research is the Life Style Index, a measure of career- versus non-career-oriented adult role aspirations. This index was constructed from a composite of several questionnaire items. Details of the construction and the *raison d'être* for the index are described in Appendix 2. The index was computed separately for each time period from freshmen to senior years, and the several indexes yielded a kind of test-retest appraisal of their own reliability. Further, since there are multiple applications of the index, Heise's (1969) technique was used to separate the reliability of the index from the stability of students' responses. When the Life Style Indexes for freshmen, sophomore and junior years were used, the reliability coefficient was .79. With the sophomore through senior indexes, the reliability coefficient was .88. Both coefficients are high.

Thus the one-month retest of freshmen, the similarity between the two freshmen classes in their questionnaire responses and the reliability coefficients for the Life Style Indexes provide a strong case. On the basis of these several kinds of evidence, we believe that the study data should be considered reliable.

How Valid Are the Study Data?

Suppose the preceding materials substantiate the consistency and relative absence of randomness in the study data. How can one be sure that the various measures used in this research on college women's attitudes and behavior did indeed reflect what they were intended to measure? Again, several types of evidence were gathered and these indicate that students seemed to respond in terms of the intent of the questions.

A central approach to dealing with validity was to establish to what extent questions about the same topic, but worded differently and asked in two separate contexts at times several months apart, would yield similar answers. Comparison of structured items on the questionnaire with open-ended interview questions about changes of major field during the four years yielded consistent responses from 94 percent of seniors. A check on the comparability of occupational choices of seniors between questionnaire and interview responses showed that 70 percent answered consistently in these two contexts. It should be stressed that this consistency is high considering that the elapsed time of about five months between the two measures also involved actual changes in occupational choice.

Still another evaluation of validity concerns a career-salience rating of seniors. Students were considered as career salient in their questionnaire responses if they answered in the career direction on both of the following two questions:

Fifteen years from now, would you like to be:

a. A housewife with no children
b. A housewife with one or more children
c. An unmarried career woman
d. A married career woman without children
e. A married career woman with children
f. Other, what?

Responses "c" and "d" and "e" were assumed to reflect a career orientation.

Assume that you are trained for the occupation of your choice, that you will marry and have children, and that your husband will earn enough so that you will never have to work unless you want to. Under these conditions, which of the following would you prefer? (Circle one):

a. to participate in clubs or volunteer work
b. to spend time on hobbies, sports or other activities
c. to work part-time in your chosen occupation
d. to work full time in your chosen occupation
e. to concentrate on home and family
f. other, explain briefly

On this question, "work part-time" and "work full-time" were considered career-oriented responses.

A second and independent assessment of career salience was made from senior interview protocols. In this case, career-salient girls were defined as those seeking to go on to graduate school and who want to fit work into their adult lives in some way, or who plan full-time work when their children are still young, or who plan to keep up in their fields working at least part-time once the children are in school. Non-career salient were defined as those students who said they see jobs as irrelevant to their later lives, or want to combine marriage with volunteer community work, or will work out of financial need not desire, or will work to fill time until marriage or until children come. A few responses were considered unratable. The two independent ratings of career salience (one from questionnaire responses, the other from interviews) were found to be associated at a Q value of .64 (Davis, 1971). This suggests that students were fairly consistent in their career orientations by senior year and that two ways of tapping this dimension yielded similar results.

Again, we compared senior year interview and questionnaire answers about a student's perception of who may have influenced her occupational choice. Such role models were grouped as "teachers and people in the occupation," or "relatives, friends and peers." From the questionnaire results, 49 percent of career-salient women said that teachers and people in the occupation had influenced them; in interviews, 68 percent of career-salient women gave this reply. The consistency of direction in response between the two contexts tends to reinforce the notion that the study data and therefore the results to be reported are valid.

Some Dilemmas in Measuring Change

Use of the panel method enables us to see the variations and the widespread shifting within the class especially in the early college years. As Feldman and Newcomb (1969, pp. 40-48) point out, it is important to know whether students become more or less alike during college on any given characteristic or dimension. From their scrutiny of numerous college student studies, they conclude that "sometimes there is increase in homogeneity, sometimes there is not" (p. 42). One needs to search further to determine which variables show such increase in homogeneity and what factors foster its occurrence.

The panel analysis lets us see both the numbers of students who change on any dimension and the direction of the change. But it carries with it the dilemma that the actual amount of change may be incorrectly assessed. Several factors enhance the possibility that this method results in overestimates of the amount of change (Harris, 1963). First, panel data over several time periods may be too refined because multiple questionings typically reveal people to be inconsistent in their responses (Kendall, 1954). Successive testings show that responses frequently shift from more extreme to less extreme and vice versa. Second, the tests themselves may be unreliable, producing different responses at different times. Third, instrument contamination can occur. Respondents may perceive that the researchers expect a particular response and alter their answers accordingly.

On the other hand, there are conditions that lead to underestimates of change. Instrument contamination can also lead to subjects recalling their earlier responses and attempting deliberately to be consistent from one time to the next (Bereiter, 1963). Added to this are the "ceiling" and "floor" constraints placed on respondents by the range of possible responses on a given test—the amount of change possible is limited by the respondent's starting point or score attained the first time. If the person began high, there is room to move downward, or if low to move upward, but the high scorer has little room to continue moving in the upward direction just as the low scorer has small opportunity to continue downward. In this study, the constraints are even greater, since the responses to most questions were dichotomized: answers were categorized as high or low, yes or no, favorable or unfavorable. Intermediate responses are obscured. Change in successive responses is only observable when the line between dichotomies is crossed, but not when it occurs within a category.

To a large extent, these conditions that enhance and

decrease the observed amount of changing counterbalance each other, so that while estimates of change for each individual may be subject to error, the amount of change for the class as a whole may be very accurate indeed. In this study, primarily because of the dichotomized responses, we may have actually underestimated the amount of change. Yet on virtually every factor studied, a sizeable portion of the class exhibits change, and the changes tend to go in both directions. Even when inconsistency is defined very narrowly, change is frequently more prevalent than consistency. Two things may be involved in this specific study: (1) that the college years are indeed a time of changeability, indecisiveness and groping, and (2) that the directional patterns observable in four years would stabilize if we continued to study the phenomenon long enough after college.

Appendix 2: The Life Style Index

The Life Style Index for each of the four years was initially built on the basis of 27 questionnaire items answered by the panel of 87 students. Each item was scored dichotomously with "one" given to the response logically related to a career-oriented outlook and "zero" given to the alternate response. Internal consistency was analyzed by assessing the relationship of each item to the total score. Chi square analyses were computed in the form of 2x2 contingency tables with a high or low score on each item and a high or low total score. Yule's Q, a measure of association defined as $Q = \frac{ad-bc}{ad+bc}$ for 2x2 tables where both variables are dichotomized, was also computed (Davis, 1971). Items that had a chi square statistical significance of at least p less than .05 and a Q value of .42 or above for all four years were retained in the final Index. In this way, 12 items from the original 27 were retained and the remainder eliminated. An internal consistency analysis of these 12 items showed that only 11 items were significantly and consistently associated with the total score through all four years of college; these 11 items were retained in the index. The scores range from 1 to 11 with a median value of 5 for the first three years and 6 for the senior year. Cutting points on each 11-item index were established at the median so that a score above the median indicates a career-salient life style and scores of r below the median indicate a non-career-salient life style. The number of students who scored above the median each year was 34 freshmen, 35 sophomores, 36 juniors and 41 seniors.

These are the 11 items in the Life Style Index; response alternatives that are bracketed indicate career salience.

1) As far as you can tell now, do you plan to continue your education after receiving a bachelor's degree?

> Yes, graduate school 1
> Yes, professional school 2
> Yes, other training 3
> No, I do not plan to continue4

2) How important do you think the following feature of an occupation has been or will be in influencing your choice of a field of work? Circle 1, 2, 3, 4 or 5 to indicate the degree of importance this work feature has for you.

Provides freedom from supervision

> Completely unimportant . . .1
> Not so important 2
> Somewhat important 3
> Quite important 4
> Very important 5

Below are some conditions under which women work. Rate yourself on these by speculating how you might feel about holding a job after marriage and graduation from college. Circle 1, 2, 3, 4 or 5 according to *whether you would want to work under each condition*.

3) No children; husband's salary adequate

> Definitely not 1

Probably not 2
Undecided 3
Probably would 4
Definitely would 5

4) One child of pre-school age; husband's salary adequate

Definitely not 1
Probably not 2
Undecided 3
Probably would 4
Definitely would 5

5) One child of pre-school age; husband's salary not adequate

Definitely not 1
Probably not 2
Undecided 3
Probably would 4
Definitely would 5

6) Two or more children of pre-school age; husband's salary not adequate.

Definitely not 1
Probably not 2
Undecided 3
Probably would 4
Definitely would 5

7) Two or more children of school age; husband's salary adequate

Definitely not 1
Probably not 2
Undecided 3
Probably would 4

Definitely would 5

8) Two or more children of school age; husband's salary not adequate

Definitely not 1
Probably not 2
Undecided 3
Probably would 4
Definitely would 5

9) Children have grown up and left home; husband's salary adequate

Definitely not 1
Probably not 2
Undecided 3
Probably would 4
Definitely would 5

10) Assume that you are trained for the occupation of your choice, that you will marry and have children, and that your husband will earn enough so that you will never have to work unless you want to. Under these conditions, which of the following would you prefer (circle one):

To participate in clubs or
volunteer work 1
To spend time on hobbies, sports
or other activities 2
To work part-time in your
chosen occupation 3
To work full-time in your chosen
occupation 4
To concentrate on home and family 5
Other (explain briefly) 6

11) Fifteen years from now, would you like to be:

> A housewife with no children 1
> A housewife with one or more children . .2
> An unmarried career woman 3
> A married career woman without children 4
> A married career woman with children . . .5
> Other: what? 6

The following hypotheses express the presumed relationship of each item to a career-salient life style as summarized in the total score:

(1) For educational values and aspirations: (a) career-salient women, should, in general, value advanced education for women and for men and (b) career-salient women should plan to continue their own education beyond college.

As it turns out, students may or may not value education as important in the abstract, their aspirations for themselves are specifically their own. Hence, only the second of these two hypotheses holds strongly and consistently all four years.

(2) In occupational aspirations: (a) career-salient women should prefer professional over non-professional work; (b) career-salient women should feel decided about which occupation to pursue and (c) career-salient women should prefer male-dominated occupations.

Nearly all the students were ambivalent and undecided about their occupational choice at some point during the four years of school and while their choices generally fall within the professional fields there was no consistent tendency for career-oriented women to prefer male-dominated fields. Therefore all three of these hypotheses had to be rejected since occupational preferences are inconsistently related to career plans.

(3) In work values (Rosenberg, 1957): (a) career-salient women should prefer work with high prestige, freedom from supervision, high income, a chance to use one's own abilities and to combine career with family, and (b) non-career-salient

women should prefer work with people, helping others, work that suits parents' success ideas, and security.

Among these, only "freedom from close supervision" is significant statistically all four years.

(4) Work motivation (Eyde, 1963): (a) career-oriented women should prefer to work more often than non-career-oriented women under each of the following conditions: when they have no children, when their children are grown and the husband's salary is adequate, with one pre-school age child regardless of husband's earnings, with two or more pre-schoolers if husband's salary is not adequate, with two or more school-age children regardless of husband's earnings.

All of these motivational conditions are significantly associated with the total score.

(5) Familial aspirations: (a) career-salient women should be willing to marry later; (b) they should be willing to have others care for their young children and (c) they should score low on Sex Role Ideology, that is, they should favor an equalitarian division of labor between husband and wife in household tasks (Hoffman, 1963).

These family attitudes do not consistently relate to the total score.

Using their Life Style Index scores as dichotomies of high and low career aspirations (with high scores above the median, and low scores at the median or below) a student was labeled as high (1) or low (2) for each year in the following way:

Freshman	Sophomore	Junior	Senior		
6-11	6-11	6-11	7-11	=	HIGH
0-5	0-5	0-5	0-6	=	LOW

Now, labeling each student's score for each year in this way leads to 16 possible combinations of 1's (high) and 2's (low) over the four times. If we look at the five student types in terms of 1's and 2's, they are defined by their change patterns as follows:

Careerists				Non-careerists				Converts				Defectors				Shifters			
Fr	So	Jr	Sr	Fr	So	Jr	Sr	Fr	So	Jr	Sr	Fr	So	Jr	Sr	Fr	So	Jr	Sr
1	1	1	1	2	2	2	2	2	2	2	1	1	2	2	2	1	2	2	1
								2	2	1	1	1	1	2	2	1	1	2	1
								2	1	1	1	1	1	1	2	1	2	1	2
																1	2	1	1
																2	1	1	2
																2	2	1	2
																2	1	2	1
																2	1	2	2

To estimate the reliability and stability coefficients using Heise's (1969) method, we designated the student scores for each year as T_1 = freshmen, T_2 = sophomores, T_3 = juniors, T_4 = seniors.

The formula for computing the reliability coefficient is

$$r_{xx} = \frac{r_{12}\,r_{23}-}{r_{13}} \quad \text{for} \quad T_1, T_2 \text{ and } T_3.$$

For T_2, T_3, and T_4, $r_{xx} = \dfrac{r_{23}\,r_{34}}{r_{24}}$.

Other reliability coefficients could be computed using T_1, T_3, T_4 or T_1, T_2, T_4 correlation values. Using T_1, T_2, T_4, the result is *.94.*

Computation of the stability coefficients is

$$s_{12} = \frac{r_{13}}{r_{23}} \quad \text{and} \quad s_{23} = \frac{r_{13}}{r_{12}} \quad \text{and} \quad s_{13} = \frac{r_{13}^{\,2}}{r_{12}\,r_{23}},$$

where r is the Pearson product moment correlation.

Since in this analysis, four-time measures of the indexes are available, stability coefficients can be computed with varying sets of three correlation coefficients. When contiguous measures are used, such as T_1, T_2, T_3 or T_2, T_3, T_4, the resulting s coefficients are higher than when non-contiguous values are used, such as T_1, T_2, T_4. The specific stability coefficients are:

S_{12} = .70 based on T_1, T_2, T_3
S_{13} = .70 based on T_1, T_2, T_3
S_{14} = .37 based on T_1, T_2, T_4
S_{23} = .89 based on T_2, T_3, T_4
S_{24} = .66 based on T_2, T_3, T_4
S_{34} = .74 based on T_2, T_3, T_4

The simple correlation coefficients between each set of Life Style Indexes are:

r_{12} = .56 r_{23} = .79
r_{13} = .56 r_{24} = .59
r_{14} = .35 r_{34} = .66

In addition, the Life Style Index values appear to meet the assumptions delineated by Heise that measurement errors are not serially correlated and that no unmeasured variable has a significant continuous impact on the LSI during the four years. This is indicated by the small difference between these two products: $r_{14}r_{23}$ = $r_{13}r_{24}$ For our data the first product is .27 and the second is .33.

References

Ainsworth, Mary D. 1962. "The Effects of Maternal Deprivation: A Review of Findings and Controversy in the Context of Research Strategy." In *Deprivation of Maternal Care: A Reassessment of Its Effects*. World Health Organization Public Health Paper No. 14, Geneva.

Almquist, Elizabeth M. 1972. "Neither White nor Male: The Disadvantaged Position of Negro Women in the Labor Force." Paper presented at the Rocky Mountain Social Science Association annual meeting, Salt Lake City.

Almquist, Elizabeth M. 1973. "The Income Losses of Working Black Women: Product of Race and Sex Discrimination." Paper presented at the American Sociological Association annual meeting, New York City.

Almquist, Elizabeth M. 1974. "Is a Good Man Hard to Find?" Working paper, Department of Sociology, North Texas State University, Denton, Texas.

Angrist, Shirley S. 1966. "Role Conception as a Predictor of Adult Female Roles," *Sociology and Social Research* 50:448-459.

Angrist, Shirley S. 1967. "Role Constellation as a Variable in Women's Leisure Activities," *Social Forces* 45:423-431.

Angrist, Shirley S., and Judith R. Lave, 1973. "Issues Surrounding Day Care," *The Family Coordinator* 22:457-464.

Angrist, Shirley S., Mark Lefton, Simon Dinitz and Benjamin Pasamanick, 1968. *Women After Treatment: A Study of Former Mental Patients and Their Normal Neighbors.* Appleton-Century-Crofts, New York.

Angrist, Shirley S., Simon Dinitz and Lois H. Molholm, 1972. "The Home as a Sheltered Workshop." Paper presented at American Sociological Association annual meeting, New Orleans.

Astin, Alexander W. 1963. "Differential College Effects on the Motivation of Talented Students to Obtain the Ph.D.," *Journal of Educational Psychology* 54:63-71.

Astin, Alexander W. 1972. "The Measured Effects of Higher Education, *Annals of the American Academy of Political and Social Science* 404:1-20.

Axelson, Leland J. 1963. "The Marital Adjustment and Marital Role Definitions of Husbands of Working and Nonworking Wives," *Marriage and Family Living* 25:189-195.

Bailyn, Lotte, 1964. "Notes on the Role of Choice in the Psychology of Professional Women," *Daedalus* 93:700-710.

Bailyn, Lotte, 1970. "Career and Family Orientations of Husbands and Wives in Relation to Marital Happiness," *Human Relations* 23:97-113.

Bailyn, Lotte, 1973. "Family Constraints on Women's Work," *Annals of the New York Academy of Sciences* 208:82-90.

Bardwick, Judith M. 1971. *Psychology of Women: A Study of Bio-Cultural Conflicts.* Harper and Row, New York.

Bardwick, Judith M. (ed.) 1972. *Readings on the Psychology of Women.* Harper and Row, New York.

Bardwick, Judith M., and Elizabeth Douvan, 1971. "Ambivalence: The Socialization of Women." In Vivian Gornick and Barbara K. Moran (eds.), *Women in Sexist Society.* Basic Books, New York, pp. 147-159.

Baruch, Grace K. 1972a. "Maternal Influence upon College Women's Attitudes Toward Women and Work," *Developmental Psychology* 6:32-37.

Baruch, Grace K. 1972b. "Maternal Role Pattern as Related to Self-Esteem and Parental Identification in College Women." Paper presented at Eastern Psychological Association annual meeting, Boston.

Bates, Frederick L. 1956. "Position, Role and Status: A Reformulation of Concepts," *Social Forces* 34:313-321.

Bayer, Alan E. 1972. "College Impact on Marriage," *Journal of Marriage and The Family* 34:600-609.

Bayer, Alan E., Jeannie T. Royer and Richard M. Webb, 1973. *Four Years After College Entry.* ACE Research Reports Volume 8, Number 1. American Council on Education, Washington, D.C.

Becker, Howard S., Blanche Geer and E. C. Hughes, 1968. *Making the Grade: The Academic Side of College Life.* Wiley, New York.

Becker, Marshall, Marilynn Katasaky and Henry Seidel, 1973. "A Follow-Up Study of Unsuccessful Applicants to Medical Schools," *Journal of Medical Education* 48:991-1001.

Benston, Margaret, 1972. "The Political Economy of Women's Liberation." In Nona Glazer-Malbin and Helen Youngelson Waehrer (eds.), *Woman in a Man-Made World.* Rand McNally, New York.

Bereiter, C. 1963. "Some Persistent Dilemmas in the Measurement of Change." In C. W. Harris (ed.), *Problems of Measuring Change.* University of Wisconsin Press, Madison, Wisconsin, pp. 3-20.

Bernard, Jessie S., 1974. *The Future of Motherhood.* Dial Press, New York, forthcoming.

Bisconti, Ann S., and Helen S. Astin, 1973. *Undergraduate and Graduate Study in Scientific Fields*. ACE Research Reports Volume 8, Number 3. American Council on Education, Washington, D.C.

Bowne, Eliza Southgate, 1888. *A Girl's Life Eighty Years Ago: Selections from the Letters of Eliza Southgate Bowne*. Charles Scribner's Sons, New York. As Reprinted and edited by Eve Merriam in *Growing Up Female in America: Ten Lives*. Dell, New York, 1971.

Broverman, Inge K., S. R. Vogel, D. M. Broverman, F. E. Clarkson and P. S. Rosenkrantz, 1972. "Sex Role Stereotypes: A Current Appraisal," *Journal of Social Issues* 28:59-78.

Buckley, John E. 1971. "Pay Difference Between Men and Women in the Same Job," *Monthly Labor Review* 94:36-39.

Burke, Kenneth, 1954. *Permanence and Change: An Anatomy of Purpose*. Hermes Publications, Los Altos, California.

Burstyn, Joan, 1973. "Educational Experiences for Women at Carnegie-Mellon University: A Brief History," *Western Pennsylvania Historical Magazine* 56:141-153.

Caplow, Theodore, 1954. *The Sociology of Work*. McGraw-Hill, New York.

Chodorow, Nancy, 1972. "Being and Doing: A Cross-Cultural Examination of the Socialization of Males and Females." In Vivian Gornick and Barbara K. Moran (eds.), *Woman in Sexist Society*. New American Library, New York, pp. 259-291.

Chronicle of Higher Education, 1974. "Enrollment of Black Freshmen Slowed This Year Study Indicates." February 11, 1974, Vol. 8, No., 19, pp. 1 and 9.

Cohen, Malcolm S. 1971. "Sex Differences in Compensation," *Journal of Human Resources*, 6:234-247.

Cronbach, Lee J. 1960. *Essentials of Psychological Testing* (2nd Edition). Harper and Row, New York.

Cross, K. Patricia, 1973. *Women in Higher Education.* American Council on Education, Washington, D.C.

Dahlström, Edmund (ed.), 1971. *The Changing Roles of Men and Women.* Beacon Press, Boston.

Davis, Fred, and Virginia Olesen, 1963. "Initiation into a Woman's Profession," *Sociometry* 26:89-101.

Davis, James A. 1965. *Undergraduate Career Decisions: Correlates of Occupational Choice.* Aldine Publishing Company, Chicago.

Davis, James A. 1966. "The Campus as a Frogpond: An Application of the Theory of Relative Deprivation to Career Decisions of College Men," *American Journal of Sociology* 72:17-31.

Davis, James A. 1971. *Elementary Survey Analysis.* Prentice-Hall, Englewood Cliffs, New Jersey.

Department of Health, Education and Welfare, 1971. "Students Enrolled for Advanced Degrees Fall 1970: Summary Data." DHEW No. 72-64, Washington, D.C.

Douvan, Elizabeth, 1960. "Sex Differences in Adolescent Character Process," *Merrill-Palmer Quarterly* 6:203-211.

Dynes, Russell R., Alfred C. Clarke and Simon Dinitz, 1956. "Levels of Occupational Aspiration: Aspects of Family Experiences as a Variable," *American Sociological Review* 21:210-218.

Ellis, Evelyn, 1952. "Social Psychological Correlates of Upward Social Mobility Among Unmarried Career Women," *American Sociological Review* 27:228-236.

Empey, Lamar T. 1958. "Role Expectations of Young Women Regarding Marriage and a Career," *Marriage and Family Living* 20:152-155.

Epstein, Cynthia F. 1970. *Woman's Place: Options and Limits in Professional Careers.* University of California Press, Berkeley, California.

Erskine, Hazel, 1971. "The Polls! Women's Roles," *The Public Opinion Quarterly* 25:275-290.

Eyde, Lorraine D. 1963. *Work Values and Background*

Factors as Predictors of Women's Desire to Work. Ohio State University Bureau of Business Research Monograph No. 108, Columbus, Ohio.

Feldman, Kenneth A., and Theodore Newcomb, 1969. *The Impact of College on Students*. Jossey-Bass, San Francisco (2 volumes).

Ferriss, Abbot L. 1971. *Indicators of Trends in the Status of Women*. Russell Sage Foundation, New York.

Fichter, Joseph H. 1972. "Marriage and Motherhood of Black Women Graduates." In Nona Glazer-Malbin and Helen Youngelson Waehrer (eds.), *Woman in a Man-Made World*. Rand-McNally, New York, pp. 203-207.

Friedan, Betty, 1963. *The Feminine Mystique*. Norton, New York.

Frieze, Irene H. 1974. "Women's Expectations for and Causal Attributions of Success and Failure." In Martha Mednick, Sandra Tangri and Lois Hoffman (eds.), *Women and Achievement: Social Psychological Perspectives*. Holt, Rinehart and Winston, New York (forthcoming).

Garland, Neal, 1970. "The Better Half? The Male in the Dual Profession Family." Paper presented at the American Sociological Association annual meeting, Washington, D.C.

Ginzberg, Eli, Sol W. Ginsberg, Sidney Axelrod and John L. Herma, 1951. *Occupational Choice: An Approach to a General Theory*. Columbia University Press, New York.

Glock, Charles Y. 1955. "Some Applications of the Panel Method to the Study of Change." In P. F. Lazarsfeld and M. Rosenberg (eds.), *The Language of Social Research*. The Free Press, New York, pp. 242-250.

Goffman, Erving, 1961. "Role Distance." In *Encounters*, Bobbs-Merrill, Indianapolis, pp. 85-152.

Gold, Sonia S. 1968. "The Power of Values III: The Professional Commitment of Educated Women." In Kurt Baier and Nicholas Rescher (eds.), *Technology and American Values*. Free Press, Glencoe, Illinois, pp. 266-293.

Gold, Sonia S. 1973. "Alternative National Goals and Women's Employment," *Science* 179:656-660.

Goldman, Nancy, 1973. "The Changing Role of Women in the Armed Forces," *American Journal of Sociology* 78:892-911.

Gordon, Nancy M., Thomas E. Morton and Ina C. Braden. 1974. "Faculty Salaries: Is There Discrimination by Sex, Race and Discipline?" *American Economic Review*, forthcoming.

Gove, Walter R. and Jeannette F. Tudor, 1973. "Adult Sex Roles and Mental Illness," *American Journal of Sociology* 78:812-835.

Gross, Edward, 1968. "Plus Ça Change . . . ? The Sexual Structure of Occupations Over Time," *Social Problems* 16:198-208.

Gump, Janice Porter, 1972. "Sex-Role Attitudes and Psychological Well-Being," *Journal of Social Issues* 28:79-92.

Haga, William J., George Graen and Fred Dansereau, Jr. 1974. "Professionalism and Role Making in a Service Organization: A Longitudinal Investigation," *American Sociological Review* 39:122-133.

Hall, Oswald, 1964. "Gender and the Division of Labor." *In Implications of Traditional Divisions Between Men's Work and Women's Work in Our Society*. Women's Bureau, Department of Labour of Canada, Ottawa.

Harmon, Lenore W. 1971. "The Childhood and Adolescent Career Plans of College Women," *Journal of Vocational Behavior* 1:45-56.

Harris, C. W. 1963. *Problems of Measuring Change*. University of Wisconsin Press, Madison, Wisconsin.

Hartley, Ruth E. 1972. "Role Models and Role Outcomes." Paper presented at Radcliffe Institute Conference on Women: Resource for Changing World, Cambridge, Massachusetts.

Hedges, Janice N., and Jeanne K. Barnett, 1972. "Working Women and the Division of Household Tasks," *Monthly Labor Review* 95:9-14.

Heise, David R. 1969. "Separating Reliability and Stability in Test-Retest Correlation," *American Sociological Review* 34:93-101.

Helson, Ravenna, 1972. "The Changing Image of the Career Woman," *Journal of Social Issues* 28:33-46.

Henry, M. and H. Renaud, 1972. "Examined and Unexamined Lives," *The Research Reporter* 7:5-8, Center for Research and Development in Higher Education, University of California, Berkeley, California.

Hoffman, Lois W. 1963. "Parental Power Relations and the Division of Household Tasks." In F. Ivan Nye and Lois W. Hoffman (eds.), *The Employed Mother in America*. Rand-McNally, Chicago, pp. 215-230.

Hoffman, Lois W. 1972. "Early Childhood Experiences and Women's Achievement Motives," *Journal of Social Issues* 28:129-156.

Holland, John L. 1959. "A Theory of Vocational Choice," *Journal of Counseling Psychology* 6:35-45.

Holland, John L. 1962. "Some Explorations of a Theory of Vocation Choice: One and Two Year Longitudinal Studies," Psychological Monographs 76, Whole No. 545.

Holland, John L. 1966. *The Psychology of Vocational Choice: A Theory of Personality Types and Model Environments*. Blaisdell, Waltham, Massachusetts.

Holland, John L. 1974. "Vocational Guidance for Everyone," *Educational Researcher* 3 (January) 9-15.

Holmstrom, Engin I., and Robert W. Holmstrom, 1974. "The Plight of the Woman Doctoral Student," *American Educational Research Journal* 11:1-17.

Horner, Matina S. 1970. "Femininity and Successful Achievement: A Basic Inconsistency." In J. Bardwick, E. M. Douvan, M. S. Horner and D. Gutmann (eds.), *Feminine Personality and Conflict*. Brooks-Cole, Belmont, California. pp. 45-74.

Horner, Matina S. 1972. "Toward an Understanding of Achievement-Related Conflicts in Women," *Journal of Social Issues* 28:157-175.

Huber, Joan, 1973. *Changing Women in a Changing Society*. University of Chicago Press, Chicago.

Jacob, Philip E. 1957. *Changing Values in College*. Harper and Brothers, New York.

Johnson, Miriam M. 1963. "Sex Role Learning in the Nuclear Family," *Child Development* 34:319-333.

Kagan, Jerome, 1973. "Check One: Male, Female." In Carol Tarvis (ed.), *The Female Experience*. Communications Research Machines Inc., Del Mar, California, pp. 51-53.

Kemper, Theodore D. 1968. "Reference Groups, Socialization and Achievement," *American Sociological Review* 33:31-45.

Kendall, Patricia L. 1954. *Conflict and Mood: Factors Affecting Stability of Response*. The Free Press, Glencoe, Illinois.

Kirk, Jerome, 1965. "Cultural Diversity and Character Change at Carnegie Tech." Unpublished Report, Carnegie Institute of Technology, Pittsburgh, Pennsylvania.

Kleinmuntz, Benjamin, 1960. "Identification of Maladjusted College Students," *Journal of Counseling Psychology* 7:209-211.

Kleinmuntz, Benjamin, 1961. "The College Maladjustment Scale (MT): Norms and Predictive Validity," *Educational and Psychological Measurement* 21:1029-1033.

Komarovsky, Mirra, 1973. "Cultural Contradictions and Sex Roles: The Masculine Case," *American Journal of Sociology* 78:873-884.

Komarovsky, Mirra, 1973a. "Some Problems in Role Analysis," *American Sociological Review* 38:649-662.

Korn, Harold A. 1967. "Careers: Choice, Chance and Inertia." In Joseph Katz (ed.), *Growth and Constraint in College Students: A Study of the Varieties of Psychological Development*. Stanford Institute for the Study of Human Problems, Stanford, California, pp. 373-421.

Krueger, Cynthia, 1968. "Do Bad Girls Become Good Nurses?" *Trans-Action* 5:31-36.

Lave, Judith R., and Shirley S. Angrist, 1974. "Factors

Affecting Child Care Expenditures of Working Mothers." Working paper, School of Urban and Public Affairs, Carnegie-Mellon University, Pittsburgh, Pennsylvania.

Lavin, David E. 1965. *The Prediction of Academic Performance: A Theoretical Analysis and Review of Research.* Russell Sage Foundations, New York.

Lazarsfeld, Paul F., Morris Rosenberg and Ann K. Pasanella, 1972. *Continuities in the Language of Social Research.* Free Press, Riverside, New Jersey.

Leibowitz, Arleen, 1972. "Women's Allocation of Time to Market and Nonmarket Activities: Differences by Education." Ph.D. Dissertation, Columbia University.

Lenski, Gerhard, 1961. *The Religious Factor: A Sociologist's Inquiry.* Doubleday, Garden City.

Lewis, Edwin, 1968. *Developing Women's Potential.* Iowa State University Press: Ames, Iowa.

Lewis, Michael, 1973. "There's No Unisex in the Nursery." In Carol Tarvis (ed.), *The Female Experience.* Communications Research Machines Inc., Del Mar, California, pp. 46-49.

Low, Seth, and Pearl G. Spindler, 1968. "Child Care Arrangements of Working Mothers in the United States." Children's Bureau Publication No. 161, Washington, D.C.

Luria, Zella, 1972. "Recent Women College Graduates: A Study of Rising Expectations." Presidential Address to New England Psychological Association annual meeting, Boston.

Maccoby, Eleanor E. 1966. "Sex Differences in Intellectual Functioning." In *The Development of Sex Differences.* Stanford University Press, Stanford, California, pp. 25-55.

Manpower Report, 1973. *Manpower Report of the President, 1973.* U.S. Department of Labor, Superintendent of Documents, Washington, D.C.

March, James G. 1972. "Model Bias in Social Action," *Review of Educational Research* 42:413-429.

Masih, Lalit K. 1967. "Career Saliency and Its Relation to Certain Needs, Interests and Job Values," *Personnel and Guidance Journal* 45:653-658.

McMillan, Marvin R. 1972. "Attitudes of College Men Toward Career Involvement of Married Women," *Vocational Guidance Quarterly* 21:8-11.

Molholm, Lois H., and Simon Dinitz, 1972. "Female Mental Patients and Their Normal Controls: A Restudy 10 Years Later," *Archives of General Psychiatry* 27:606-610.

Neugarten, Bernice, 1972. "Education and the Life Cycle," *School Review* 80:209-218.

Newcomb, Theodore M., Kathryn E. Koenig, Richard Flacks and Donald P. Warwick, 1967. *Persistence and Change: Bennington College and Its Students After 25 Years.* Wiley, New York.

Oppenheimer, Valerie Kincaide, 1968. "The Sex-Labeling of Jobs," *Industrial Relations* 7:219-234.

Oppenheimer, Valerie Kincaide, 1970. *The Female Labor Force in the United States: Demographic and Economic Factors Governing Its Growth and Changing Composition.* Population Monograph Series, No. 5, University of California, Institute of International Studies, Berkeley, California.

Oppenheimer, Valerie Kincaide, 1973. "Demographic Influence on Female Employment and the Status of Women," *American Journal of Sociology* 78:946-961.

Orden, Susan R., and Norman M. Bradburn, 1969. "Working Wives and Marriage Happiness," *American Journal of Sociology* 74:392-407.

Panos, R. J., A. W. Astin and J. A. Creager, 1967, *National Norms for Entering College Freshman—Fall 1967.* ACE Research Reports, American Council on Education, Washington, D.C.

Parsons, Talcott, 1954. "Age and Sex in the Social Structure of the United States." In *Essays in Sociological Theory.* Free Press, Glencoe, Illinois, pp. 89-103.

Perrella, Vera C. 1968. "Women and the Labor Force," *Monthly Labor Review* 91:1-12.

Perrucci, Carolyn C. 1970. "Minority Status and the Pursuit of Professional Careers of Women in Science and Engineering," *Social Forces* 49:245-258.

Plant, Walter T. 1962. *Personality Changes Associated with a College Education.* U.S. Office of Health, Education and Welfare, Washington, D.C.

Plub, Dorothy A., and George B. Dowell, 1961. *The Magnificent Enterprise: A Chronicle of Vassar College.* Vassar College, Poughkeepsie, New York.

Poloma, Margaret, 1970. "The Myth of the Egalitarian Family: Familial Roles and the Professionally Employed Wife." Paper presented at the American Sociological Association annual meeting, Washington, D.C.

Psathas, George, 1968. "Toward a Theory of Occupational Choice for Women," *Sociology and Social Research* 52:253-268.

Rabin, A. I. 1970. "The Sexes: Ideology and Reality in the Israeli Kibbutz." In G. H. Seward and R. C. Williamson (eds.), *Sex Roles in Changing Society.* Random House, New York, pp. 285-307.

Rand, Lorraine, 1971. "Masculinity or Femininity? Differentiating Career-Oriented and Homemaking-Oriented College Freshman Women." In Athena Theodore (ed.), *The Professional Woman.* Schenkman, Cambridge, Massachusetts, pp. 156-166.

Rapoport, Rhona, and Robert Rapoport, 1971. *Dual Career Families.* Penguin Books, Middlesex, England.

Reisman, David, 1973. "Observations on Contemporary College Students—Especially Women." In Peter K. Manning (ed.), *Youth: Divergent Perspectives.* Wiley, New York, pp. 136-154.

Roberts, Ron E. 1971. *The New Communes: Coming*

Together in America. Prentice-Hall, Englewood Cliffs, New Jersey.

Roe, Anne, 1963. *The Making of a Scientist.* Dodd Mead, New York. Reprint of 1953 edition.

Rosenberg, Morris, 1957. *Occupations and Values.* Free Press, Glencoe, Illinois.

Ross, Aileen D. 1958. "Control and Leadership in Women's Groups: An Analysis of Philanthropic Money Raising Activity," *Social Forces* 37:124-131.

Rossi, Alice S. 1965. "Women in Science: Why So Few?" *Science* 148:1196-1202.

Rossi, Alice S. 1967. "The Roots of Ambivalence in American Women." Paper presented at Continuing Education Conference, Oakland University, Michigan.

Rossi, Alice S. 1968. "Transition to Parenthood," *Journal of Marriage and the Family* 30:26-39.

Rushing, William A. 1964. "Adolescent-Parent Relationships and Mobility Aspirations," *Social Forces* 43:157-166.

Safilios-Rothschild, 1974. *Women and Social Policy.* Prentice-Hall, Englewood Cliffs, New Jersey.

Sarbin, Theodore R. 1954. "Role Theory." In Gardner Lindzey (ed.), *Handbook of Social Psychology.* Addison-Wesley, Cambridge, Massachusetts, Volume 1, pp. 223-258.

Sawhill, Isabel V. 1973. "The Economics of Discrimination Against Women: Some New Findings," *Journal of Human Resources* 8:383-396.

Scott, Anne F. 1971. *The American Woman: Who Was She?* Prentice-Hall, Englewood Cliffs, New Jersey.

Scott, John F. 1965. "The American College Sorority: Its Role in Class and Ethnic Endogamy," *American Sociological Review* 30:514-527.

Searls, Laura G. 1966. "Leisure Role Emphasis of College Graduate Homemakers," *Journal of Marriage and the Family* 28:77-82.

Senter, R. J. 1969. *Analysis of Data.* Scott, Foresman, Glenview, Illinois.

Seward, G. H. 1945. "Cultural Conflict and the Feminine Role," *Journal of Social Psychology* 22:177-194.

Shab, Fred, 1967. "Southern College Women: A Comparison of Arts and Science Majors with Education Majors," *American Association of University Women Journal* 60:142-144 and 148.

Sherr, Lynn, and Jurate Kazickas, 1973. *The Liberated Woman's Appointment Calendar, 1974.* Universe Books: New York.

Shibutani, Tamotsu, 1955. "Reference Groups as Perspectives," *American Journal of Sociology* 60:562-568.

Siegel, Alberta E., and Elizabeth Curtis, 1963. "Familial Correlates of Orientation Toward Future Employment Among College Women," *Journal of Educational Psychology* 44:33-37.

Slocum, Walter L., and Lamar T. Empey, 1956. *Occupational Planning by Young Women.* Agricultural Experiment Station Bulletin No. 568, Pullman, Washington.

Smith, Constance, and Anne Freedman, 1972. *Voluntary Associations: Perspectives on the Literature.* Harvard University Press, Cambridge, Massachusetts.

Smuts, Robert W. 1960. "The Female Labor Force: A Case Study in the Interpretation of Historical Statistics," *Journal of the American Statistical Association* 55:71-79.

Smuts, Robert W. 1971. *Women and Work in America.* Schocken Books, New York.

Stanford Committee on the Education and Employment of Women in the University, 1972. *The Stanford Woman in 1972: A Study of Undergraduate Choice of Academic Fields and Future Occupations.* Stanford University, Stanford, California.

Stern, George G. 1970. *People in Context: Measuring Person-Environment Congruence in Education and Industry.* Wiley, New York.

Strong, Edward K., Jr. 1955. *Vocational Interests 18 Years After College.* University of Minnesota Press, Minneapolis.

Suelzle, Marijean, 1970. "Women in Labor," *Trans-Action* 8:50-58, November-December.

Super, Donald E., 1953. "A Theory of Vocational Development," *The American Psychologist* 8:185-190.

Suter, Larry E., and Herman P. Miller, 1973. "Income Differences Between Men and Career Women," *American Journal of Sociology* 78:962-974.

Sweet, James A. 1973. *Women in the Labor Force.* Seminar Press, New York.

Szalai, Alexander, 1972. *The Use of Time: Daily Activities of Urban and Suburban Populations in Twelve Countries.* Mouton, The Hague.

Thielens, Wagner, Jr. 1971. "Teacher-Student Interaction, Higher Education: Student Viewpoint." In Encyclopedia of Education 9:54-63.

Thompson, Barbara, and Angela Finlayson, 1963. "Married Women Who Work in Early Motherhood." *British Journal of Sociology* 14:150-168.

Toews, Lorette, 1972. "Self-Hatred in College Women: Sex Role Stereotypes and Same-Sex Affiliation." Ph.D. Dissertation, University of Alberta, Edmonton, Alberta.

Turner, Ralph H., 1964. "Some Aspects of Women's Ambition," *American Journal of Sociology* 70:270-285.

Useem, Ruth Hill, 1966. *What Does Society Expect Higher Education to Do for Women: Who Knows and Who Cares?* Current Issues in Higher Education, Association for Higher Education 21st National Conference Proceedings, pp. 136-140. National Education Association, Washington, D.C.

U.S. Bureau of the Census, 1973. *Census of Population 1970: Subject Reports, Occupational Characteristics.* Final Report PC (2)-7A.

U.S. Bureau of the Census, 1973a. *Census of Population 1970: General Social and Economic Characteristics.* Final Report PC(1) United States Summary.

U.S. Department of Labor, 1969. "A Summary of Facts About Absenteeism and Labor Turnover." Prepared by U.S. Department of Labor, Women's Bureau.

U.S. Office of Education, 1971. "Earned Degrees Conferred 1970-71." National Center for Educational Statistics, U.S. Office of Education, Washington, D.C.

Veblen, Thorstein, 1899. *The Theory of the Leisure Class.* The Macmillan Company, New York. Reprinted by Augustus M. Kelly Publishers, New York, 1965.

Vincent, Clark, 1966. "Implications of Changes in Male-Female Role Expectations for Interpreting M-F Scores," *Journal of Marriage and Family* 28:196-199.

Waldman, Elizabeth, and Kathryn R. Gover, 1971. "Children of Women in the Labor Force," *Monthly Labor Review* 94:19-25.

Waldman, Elizabeth, and Kathryn R. Gover, 1972. "Marital and Family Characteristics of the Labor Force," *Monthly Labor Review* 95:4-8.

Walker, Kathryn E. 1972. "Time Use for Care of Family Members." Working paper, Use-of-Time Research Project, Department of Consumer Economics and Public Policy, Cornell University, Ithaca, New York.

Walker, Kathryn E. 1973. "Effect of Family Characteristics on Time Contributed for Household Work by Various Members." Paper presented at American Home Economics Association annual meeting, Atlantic City, New Jersey.

Wallace, Walter L. 1970. "The Perspective of College Women." In Athena Theodore (ed.), *The Professional Woman.* Schenkman, Cambridge, Massachusetts, pp. 381-396.

Watley, Donivan J., and Rosalyn Kaplan, 1971. "Career or Marriage? Aspirations and Achievements of Able Young Women," *Journal of Vocational Behavior* 1:29-43.

Webster, Harold, Mervin Freedman and Paul Heist, 1962. "Personality Changes in College Students." In Nevitt Sanford (ed.), The American College: A Psychological and Social Interpretation of the Higher Learning. Wiley, New York, pp. 811-846.

White, Becky J. 1959. "The Relationship of Self-Concept and Parental Identification to Women's Vocational Interests," *Journal of Counseling Psychology* 1:202-206.

White, Kinnard, 1967. "Social Background Variables Related to Career Commitment of Women Teachers," *Personnel and Guidance Journal*, 45:648-652.

Wiggins, Lee M. 1973. *Panel Analysis*. Jossey-Bass, San Francisco.

Wohl, Lisa Cronin, 1973. "Liberating Ma Bell," *MS Magazine* 2:52-54 and 92-97, No. 5.

Women's Bureau, 1966. *College Women Seven Years After Graduation: Resurvey of Women Graduates, Class of 1957*. U.S. Department of Labor, Women's Bureau Bulletin 292, Washington, D.C.

Zissis, Cecelia, 1962. "The Relationship of Selected Variables to Career-Marriage Plans of University Freshman Women." Ph.D. Dissertation, Department of Education, University of Michigan, Ann Arbor, Michigan.

Name Index

Subject Index